Believe It Or Not

BILL WILLIAMS

Believe It Or Not

Bill Williams

with

Ian James Bradford

MEMORIES
OF MY LIFE

*To Jill, for being my biggest supporter over the years;
to my sons Nick and James – I'm very proud of you, lads
– and also, of course, to Claire.*

Acknowledgements

I PARTICULARLY want to thank Ian James Bradford from the ghostwriting service *Memories of My Life* for the care he has taken in helping me to put my story down in book form.

I am also grateful to Tony Saunders and John Barton for rummaging through their memories and programme collections, and to Tony Lawless and Barry Fenn for the loan of their Maidstone United scrapbooks.

Front cover photograph: Steve Terrell
Cover design: Ciaran Marshall

All photographs are taken from the author's private collection and must not be reproduced without asking nicely first.

Contents

Foreword

by Peter Taylor

I FIRST met Bill Williams in 1982 when I arrived at Maidstone United towards the end of my playing career. Having previously turned out for Crystal Palace under Malcolm Allison, Spurs managed by Keith Burkinshaw and the national side led by Don Revie, I wasn't entirely sure what to expect from the relatively unknown boss of a semi-professional outfit.

But it soon became clear that Bill was a great manager to play for. He knew the game. He wanted to produce good football teams. He gave you space if he trusted you and your ability and he treated me exactly the way I wanted to be treated after a decent professional career (although I don't doubt he was much stricter with the younger players). He worked very hard at his job and had good contacts so could always find a player if the team needed one. He was successful and won leagues. He was very tall.

However, as you are about to read, Bill is not only a big man but also a big character. I will never forget one particular night of training at London Road. Disappointed with some of the players' attitudes and performances, Bill wanted to squeeze a little bit more from the squad. As our leader he called all the players together to address us as a group and took up his position in the middle of the circle. Towards the end of our dressing down, Bill became a little more wound up and slammed the football he had been holding into the turf to make his point. He carried on talking as the ball ballooned into the air and yes, you've guessed it, it fell from the sky smack on top of his head. Bill just started laughing and so did the rest of us. It was a great way to finish the chat and keep the spirits high.

I wouldn't particularly have wanted to face Bill in a crunching tackle during his playing days – who would – but as a manager he was a gentle giant who said the right things and stayed in control. Thankfully Maidstone United in my time were a very good team and he didn't have to lose his temper too many times, but we were always aware that he could put his foot down hard if he needed to.

I was playing for Leyton Orient when Bill approached me in 1982. I went to the club to speak to him and decided to finish at Orient and play non-league with Maidstone. It just felt right. Although I was persuaded back into the League by Exeter City in 1983 that didn't last long and Bill took me back the following year. I was part-time for Maidstone but I found myself enjoying my football more than I did in my latter years playing full-time.

That, frankly, was largely down to Bill Williams.

Peter Taylor
September 2013

1

Come On You Stones

IT HAS just turned half past four on a Saturday afternoon. It is lashing down, and my beloved Maidstone United are five-nil down at home.

Believe it or not though, I am beaming. Choruses of *Come On You Stones* bounce between the terraces and in all my time in football, never have I heard supporters chant so joyously as their team is being thrashed. But as every soaked person in the ground here today knows, this is no ordinary football match.

It is July 2012. Following a twenty-four year exile from Kent's county town, the club has finally returned to a spanking new ground and are christening The Gallagher Stadium with a showpiece friendly against Brighton and Hove Albion. Regardless of the score and regardless of the weather, games don't come much more special than this.

Having been involved with the club in some capacity or

other for more than forty years – and as Chief Executive and Director of Football at the time of writing – I had tasked myself with finding a team for us to play against at our official unveiling. I obviously wanted to attract a decent-sized club and after speaking to Charlton, their officials seemed quite happy to help us cut the ribbons and their players weren't too bothered about filling their boots with bits of black rubber.

However, with the match-day programmes virtually on their way to the printers, Charlton pulled out: their first team had been offered a trip to Spain and after a long hard think for what was probably all of about four seconds, they decided they would rather spend a week on a Costa than an afternoon in Maidstone.

Understandably, Charlton's withdrawal was a hammer blow to our plans and there was a time in the pre-season when it looked very much as though we wouldn't have a showpiece match at all. A panic-stricken CEO spent a couple of weeks phoning around to call in all the favours he possibly could, and I have to say they were very desperate hours.

To be completely honest, I had just about given up hope, when one Sunday afternoon I was barbecuing in the back garden and Jill appeared with the telephone: a certain Mr Gus Poyet wanted a word. Naturally I thought it was a wind up, but sure enough, there on the other end of the line was the unmistakable Uruguayan offering to bring the entire Seagulls' first team up to the Gallagher.

I'm not sure if it was joy or relief but if Gus had been in front of me, I would have picked him up and given him the biggest hug and kiss any man has had for a very long time. Luckily for Gus, Jill copped it instead, although she couldn't quite understand the need for all my excitement. Even so, she did say she hoped I received a few more of those type of phone calls over the years ahead.

So I can tell you that I was the most relieved person in the stadium on our big day. There had been a tremendous amount of hard work by many people in the months leading up to the match, and the preparation had been meticulous. Weeks had been spent planning the event with the local authorities, the council, fire brigade and police, and our event management blueprint was as good as you would find at our level of football.

It was quite surreal wandering around the ground: we had finally reached a point which so many people thought they'd never see. The day was a new experience for everyone at the club, from the board, through the management to the spectators and everyone worked their socks off to make sure it would live long in the memory. Personally, I have been involved in many great footballing occasions during my time but that day – although it was a relief when it was over – will always stand right up there.

It had been a long haul for the club but at last the future looked bright. It had also been a fair journey for me too, and the Stones' homecoming got me thinking about the miles I had clocked up in the name of football.

Now what's that famous quote? Ah, yes: 'Sometimes you have to look back to see just how far you've come...'

2

Not to the Manor Born

PICTURE a young lad booting a ball across the sweeping lawn of a magnificent manor house. The pile, which stands on a private road in the swanky Surrey suburbs, is called White Oaks. The boy is me: William Thomas Williams.

Now then, before we go any further, let's get the whole 'William Williams' thing out of the way...

I have to say that I really don't know what my mother was thinking. But I am sure of two things: firstly, that I was named after Uncle Billy; one of my Mum's nine brothers and sisters, and secondly, if you've been lumbered with a first name that matches your second name, customs officials tend to throw you a sarcastic scowl which seems to say: 'Are you having a laugh, mate?' I daresay Neville Neville and Duran Duran get the same treatment.

Actually, scores of men down the decades have been christened William Williams by their mum, including several

Welsh rugby players; an American poet, a New York disc jockey, two New Zealand bishops and the last man executed in Minnesota for murder. Football-wise, there was a Billy Williams who played full-back for West Brom and England in the late 1800s, a William Williams who turned out for Blackpool and Everton during the 1920s and, more recently, a Bill Williams who played for (and decorated houses around) Stockport in the 1980s. No wonder the crowd never sang *There's Only One Bill Williams* when I was on the pitch.

That wonderful thing called Google also tells me that a Sir William Williams (sounds good, doesn't it?) was knighted for his work as an MP in the early 1700s. A radical Welsh politician of the same name also went into parliament, although his campaigning career was fatally unsaddled in 1865, when the silly Billy fell off his horse in Hyde Park.

Much later, in the 1960s, there was an American television and film actor called Herman August Wilhelm Katt. So what, I hear you ask? Well, Herr Katt decided to abandon his given name and adopt the screen moniker of Bill Williams; a move which made him so popular, he was awarded a star on the Hollywood Walk of Fame. One can only assume he made the change after word had reached Tinseltown of a promising young footballer in England, and he thought he'd catch a ride on my coat-tails. Either that or Herman the German was fed up with everyone taking the Matt Le Tiss.

William Williams, I'm told, is also the real name of Fat Tony, the pistol-wielding, cigar-chomping gangster boss of the Springfield Mafia in *The Simpsons*.

But best of all, there's an American town on Route 66 in Arizona called Williams, which is named in honour of William 'Old Bill' Williams, a master fur trapper who lived and died in that neck of the woods during the late eighteenth and early nineteenth century. In addition to an eight-foot tall bronze statue, the town is littered with dedications to this famous Davy Crockett-type character and believe it or not you can check out the view from the top of Bill Williams Mountain, sail a boat along Bill Williams River, walk your dog in Bill Williams Park and buy some candy and a kettle at the Bill Williams Five and Dime.

I've not been to the town myself – Jill stopped off a few years ago on her way to Las Vegas and bought a Bill Williams Wanted Dead or Alive poster, like you do if you're married to me – so I'm not exactly sure if it's possible to prop up the Bill Williams Bar while washing down a Bill Williams Cheeseburger with a Bill Williams Beer, but I would certainly like to imagine so. Whatever, enough of that Old Bill; let's get back to me.

My fantastic upbringing at White Oaks certainly had an air of *Upstairs, Downstairs* about it, and looking back I wouldn't have been particularly surprised if I'd walked into the kitchen one day to find Gordon Jackson chuntering about the new footman while polishing the family silver.

The estate in Esher was owned not by my parents but by the Gibbs family, and at the time of my birth – 23 August, 1942 – my mother, Isabella, had been their cook and housekeeper for twenty years since leaving her hometown of Newcastle.

I naturally grew up believing I had entered the world in that grand residence, but there is nothing like your family for keeping secrets and later in life I discovered that although I was indeed born in Esher, I had not arrived in splendid style at all but in a council house in Farm Road. It was a mystery that my mother took to her grave – I only found out after she had passed away – so I shall never know the reason why I was *not* to the manor born.

My father, christened Kenneth although everyone called him 'Larry', the nickname he picked up in the army, was a soldier in the Welsh Guards. He married my mother rather late in life, which obviously meant they were not a young couple when they had me. I therefore remained an only child but they were very doting parents and I vividly remember being told that everything I did was wonderful...

Despite having no brothers or sisters I never felt short of companionship thanks to Mr and Mrs Gibbs' two sons; Michael, who was a couple of years older than me, and Peter, who was the same age. Their dad Pip was an insurance underwriter at Lloyd's Marine and a former Oxford Blue, and he would often join the three of us in the garden for a kickabout.

It was in the vast grounds of White Oaks that I spent so many happy hours. Situated on the fringe of Sandown Park racecourse, the house had a swimming pool and an orchard and was home to chickens, rabbits and the Gibbs' lovely bulldog, Buffer. He had come to the family as a pup and gave us boys endless days of fun as we chased each other round and round the garden.

I can still recall the wild stormy night when one of the huge oak trees the house was named after got spliced down the middle by a forking great bolt of lightning. I also remember the air raid shelter at the bottom of the garden and hearing Mum's wartime stories of how the family would bolt to its sanctuary, while Hitler's doodlebugs en route to London were attacked by the AK-AK guns scattered across Sandown Park.

Despite standing knee-high to a whippersnapper, I still did my bit in the war by playing a part in Operation Pied Piper, the wholesale evacuation of children fittingly named after the rather menacing German folk character. Like three million other kids, I found myself standing at a train station labelled like a piece of luggage, wearing a mac and a cap and carrying a small suitcase in one hand and a gas mask in the other.

I was whisked away from White Oaks to the Welsh mining village of Onllwyn, to stay with my grandparents, my lovely Aunt Enid and her son David Jones (who also went on to become a professional footballer, turning out in goal for Coventry City).

But no sooner had I settled in Wales my mother arrived along with Mrs Gibbs and her two sisters, and to this day I still have no idea how we all managed to squeeze into that tiny terraced house. They were wonderful times though and it was remarkable how such a strong bond developed between people from such wildly different backgrounds.

I enjoyed going to school in Onllwyn although one painful lesson is certainly hard to forget: myself and half-a-dozen other lads were caught playing truant and our punishment was to stand in front of the class as the teacher striped a cane across our backsides. My walk to school each morning also evokes strong memories, and I will always be able to picture the incongruous sight of the miners swapping shifts, with the fresh gang marching down the hill all smart and clean passing the stale ones labouring up it as black as Newgate's knocker.

My Welsh grandmother was stone deaf but always wanted to know what everyone was saying. Hearing aids were in the early stages of development so over our games of Whist and Bridge in the parlour, scraps of paper would pass between the family so we could scribble little messages to keep Nan Williams up to speed. After a game of cards Granddad Williams would often keep us entertained until bedtime – he was miner but also a great pianist – or perhaps Aunt Enid would spin us a yarn. She was a real character and later in life wrote scripts for the Welsh comedian Max Boyce. Needless to say, I think I inherited my love of storytelling from Aunt Enid.

A stocky, big-bosomed nurse with rather hard features, Enid was notorious for her manly hands, the result of all the physical work she did in the Valleys as a young girl. One rather amazing trick she performed on a weekly basis would be to remove the Sunday joint from the oven without gloves. As you can imagine, she was actually very embarrassed about her shovels and would hide them behind her back whenever she could. Thinking about it now, she would have made a decent goalkeeper if she'd been a couple of feet taller.

The first story I remember Aunt Enid telling me concerned Eyan, one of the Mitchell lads who lived next door. A small boy with a slightly deformed back, Eyan was motorbike mad and saved up for ages to buy his very own two-wheeled chariot: a 250 Matchless Twin to be precise. Eyan was naturally very keen to show it off to the neighbours who, in turn, were naturally very keen to have a nose at his impressive purchase...

Eyan's plan was to fly down the road to the colliery then back up the hill to the house. As he proudly revved his bike on the 'start' line, Enid decided the audience would enjoy a much better view of the spectacle from her bedroom window, so as Eyan's revs grew shriller and shriller she ushered the assembled neighbours upstairs.

It took a minute or two for them all to get settled, by which time Eyan was nowhere to the seen. 'Oooh,' purred Enid in her low Welsh twang, 'there's quickly our Eyan goes on his motorbike', and with another glance up and down the road, the crestfallen posse shuffled back downstairs to the parlour.

They were soon interrupted by a frantic knock on the door. It was Mrs Mitchell. 'Oooh, come quickly and see our Eyan,' she said, before explaining how Eyan hadn't flown down the road faster than the speed of sight, but had kicked the bike onto its back wheel, pulled down hard on the left handlebar and shot straight through his own front door. Mrs Mitchell, it turned out, had discovered both man and machine largely burnt out in her living room fireplace.

When the war came to an end everyone must have made major changes to their lives, not that I noticed any difference back at White Oaks. Rationing was in place, of course, but it didn't seem to affect the wealthy Gibbs family too much. Their mansion was a beautiful old building and on the kitchen wall hung a large butler's bell box bearing the name of each room. When one of the Gibbs wanted something it would rattle and buzz and off to the required room Mum would trot. Mind you, that box stopped ringing quite so often as she grew older.

Mum was a wonderful cook and even as a young boy I remember her telling me that if, one day, I was going to play football for Newcastle United, I would need to eat sensible food and most definitely not take up smoking. She, meanwhile, chuffed sixty a day and sank a few gin and tonics for good measure, so I guessed she wasn't intending to turn out for The Magpies herself.

Dad, like his father, was a miner from the Valleys and as hard as old nails. He never liked football and believed it was a game played by 'poofs'. Being a typical Welshman though, rugby in his mind was a different sport altogether.

Somewhat sadly, Dad didn't watch me play until very late in my career, after I signed for The Stones in the Seventies. He eventually came to an away match at the Metropolitan Police's ground at Imber Court, but even then spent most of the second half in the bar. Still, I do know he was tremendously proud that I had become a professional footballer.

I was twelve when Dad was discharged from the army. Part of his resettlement meant that we had to leave White Oaks for pastures new. And what a shock to my system that was: kissing goodbye to a mini stately home and saying hello to a two-up, two-down on a council estate was, you could say, like leaving Downton Abbey and moving into 23 Railway Cuttings.

Summer in the council house wasn't so bad but the winters were very uncomfortable, not least of all because our only loo was now situated in a shed halfway down the garden. There was no central heating back then and the coal fire in the living room was our only source of warmth. Ice would form on the inside of the windows and we'd pile layer upon layer when a call of nature made it necessary to brave the freezer-come-toilet.

As I said Mum would smoke sixty-odd a day and Dad would get through at least twenty himself, so I guess I was passively chain-smoking as a child. And when you add the fumes coughing out of the open fire, it was no surprise to anyone when I was diagnosed asthmatic.

Being the new kid on the council-owned block, it wasn't long before I got into my first scrap and quite a few fights followed, usually when I failed to turn the other cheek to rude comments about the posh boy from No.19. Still, sparring with the local lads certainly taught me how to look after myself.

As a civilian my father opened a boot repair business above a stable block, which housed the horses employed on the hayroll of United Dairies. I think the room must have been where all the straw was originally stored. Dad employed half-a-dozen workers and all but one was deaf and dumb - not an acceptable term today I'm sure – so he learnt sign language. It was, for a time, quite a prosperous little business I think.

I would often pop in after school to help Dad get the orders out, but in the evenings I would head straight up to the Lower Green Recreation Ground to watch the older boys playing football. Being only thirteen at the time I was too young to join in, but I would fetch the balls when they were hoofed hither and thither and it soon got noticed that I could dribble and kick so I was invited to play the occasional game.

Before long I was one of the first to be picked and suddenly the posh boy had earned his stripes: he could hold his own on the football field with the older lads and, if called upon, was handy with his fists.

Having settled into my new neighbourhood I was invited to join a small-time gang. One of the lads that hung around, Arthur Bridger, came from a family of ten, which as an only child I found fascinating; watching them need two sittings for supper was a sight to behold. Arthur had four sisters, three of whom were older than us, and as embarrassing as it is to admit now, those girls were responsible for giving the pair of us our first *real* kissing lessons...

Dull moments were rare on the council estate and I enjoyed some terrific times. We never locked the door at home so ours was always an open house, particularly on Saturday nights when a party would be thrown in the small front room. Apart from the chairs, which were pushed against the walls, all the furniture would be stacked in the garden and Mum and Dad would knock out tunes on the piano as the neighbours danced around slurping and spilling beer. The fun would usually run into the small hours, but we always knew it was time to call it a night when Dad began reciting passages from Shakespeare.

The whole family was very musical and my grandfather was a tremendous pianist who performed at various miner welfare clubs. I'll always remember his wonderful version of

The Laughing Clown, and if he'd known what I'd end up doing for a living, he could have dedicated it to some of the referees I would not be amused by.

I never learnt to play the black and white keys myself which I have regretted over the years, but I did buy my first guitar when I was about thirteen and began playing in skiffle groups and local rock bands. I still have a guitar today but have to say that I haven't really improved much, as my family and neighbours will no doubt confirm.

By the time I was fourteen I had built quite a reputation as a strong athlete and a skilful footballer: I had turned out for Surrey and was having trials for England Schools plus, of course, I was now first pick on the Rec. Unfortunately there weren't any good teams playing nearby: Esher, after all, is a posh place where only rugby and cricket is played to a high level. I would therefore cycle over to Jill's – we had met at school as twelve-year-olds – which was near Hampton Court on the boundary of East and West Molesey. They had a team in the Surrey Senior League and an Under-18 side in the Surrey Minor League, and one of the gang I was running around with in Esher was playing for their youth side, and he asked me to join them.

Most of the lads were seventeen and although I had only just turned fifteen when I pitched up with my boots, being six feet two and rather skinny made me hard to miss. I was also better than most of them (not that I've ever been conceited, of course) and it wasn't long before a few football scouts came knocking.

The first major talent-spotter to show interest was a man named Frank Amos, an ex-pro representing Arsenal Football Club. Mr Amos came to the house one day to speak with my parents who I have to say weren't too pleased at the prospect of me playing professionally as Mum, in particular, wanted me to stay on at school then get an apprenticeship in a drawing office or a bank.

Nevertheless I got my way and off I went for a trial. I did well and was invited back to Highbury but to this day I can't tell you exactly what happened, only to say that along with Arsenal and West Ham, Portsmouth were also showing an interest. I can only guess that Mum took a fancy to Pompey's sweet-talking Reg Flewin, as all talk of apprenticeships suddenly flew out of the window.

Which reminds me of one of the many jokes that were told at Reg's expense during my time at Fratton Park: 'I opened the window one day and Reg Flew-in.' It was a silly gag, obviously, and we never poked fun at Reg when he was within earshot, but that probably had something to do with the fact that his nickname was 'Bluto'.

Whatever, with Mum and Dad now on side, it was agreed that I could follow my footballing dreams with Bluto – sorry, I mean Reg – at Portsmouth Football Club.

I was on my way.

3

Come in 007, Your Bath is Ready

I T WAS a bright and thrilling Friday in April 1958 when I signed forms to become an apprentice with Portsmouth.

I'd already been down to Fratton Park a couple of times to look around, but being sweet sixteen, the club needed Mum and Dad to sanction the paperwork on my behalf. Unfortunately they both had work commitments on the day I was due to sign, so it was agreed that I would go down to Hampshire on the Friday to watch the home game against Manchester United, stay at my new digs until Wednesday, come home on the Thursday to collect my belongings then go back the following Friday to complete the deal. I felt so proud being picked up at Portsmouth train station and taken to the ground to see the dressing rooms for the first time.

When I arrived the next day for the big match against United, I was invited up to the directors' box to watch the ground slowly fill as the teams warmed up. I'd been paired with a lad named Darby Watts, the club's eldest groundstaff boy (which was the name given to apprentices back then). Darby was busily pointing out the strengths and weaknesses of both sets of players and I remember being extremely impressed by his football knowledge. (Mind you, Darby momentarily forgot his soccer savvy some years later: according to the 1971-72 *Rothman's Football Yearbook*, he was sent off as Guildford's captain during an FA Cup tie against Cheshunt after just *two* minutes. Eat your heart out Vinnie Jones.)

The game against Manchester United was an absolute cracker and ended three goals apiece. Of all the great players on the park that afternoon one stood head and shoulders above the rest; a tall, skinny lad playing for Pompey named Derek Dougan. Now Dougan was only nineteen at the time but he absolutely terrorised the Reds' defence, scored the second and rattled the post on the final whistle.

I can still smell the wintergreen and feel the steam billowing from the bath in the dressing room after the game. Teams would share a communal bath in those days, of course, which was not the most hygienic thing to do but went unquestioned. It certainly came as a relief to everyone when showers became commonplace, followed by individual slipper baths and the abolition of the shared tub altogether. Nevertheless, the bath at Loftus Road played a starring role in two enjoyable episodes later in my career at QPR...

The ground at Loftus Road is adjacent to the BBC's White City studios and celebrities and other well-to-dos would often pop in for a snifter at our clubhouse under the main stand. One afternoon, a brigade from *Queen* magazine trooped in, wanting to photograph a bunch of leggy models flouncing around in come-hither frocks.

After using various spots around the ground, the snappers decided to wrap the shoot in the dressing rooms, with the players laughing naked in the bath and the glamour girls sat around poolside, their hair and dresses windswept by half-a-dozen freezing cold fans (that's half-a-dozen freezing cold electric fans, not half-a-dozen freezing cold QPR fans).

Sitting in such a dreadful draft naturally left the poor girls with more than just a chill on their chest – they were actually freezing to death, probably – so when the cameras stopped clicking they sensibly took our advice and jumped in the steamy water to join us, where they soon found themselves thoroughly defrosted...

The second unforgettable bath time I enjoyed at QPR came soon afterwards, when I played against a Showbiz XI in front of 16,000 spectators (I doubt you'd get that many these days to watch some bloke off *Hollyoaks* doing keepy-uppy). Most of the opposing celebrities were not exactly household names, as you'd expect, but after the game something happened to me that millions of women around the globe would happily give their handbag *and* their shoe collection for – yes, I shared a bath with a young Sean Connery.

Without those filthy old communal tubs then, I wouldn't be able to brag over a pint in the Spitfire Lounge today that during my playing career, I bathed with a host of famous footballers, a deluge of delicious models, and James Bond 007.

But all that was a little way off. Back at Fratton Park my first job was to help the groundsman and the two other apprentices scrub the stadium's fifty-two toilets and sweep its huge terraces. It was non-stop: we worked from nine to four, shot back to our digs to change then returned at six to train.

But we had some great fun along the way and I particularly remember good times with Alfie; the fat-old-smelly boiler man who spent all his time in the cellar stoking coal to keep the ground above freezing. More than once we had to rescue him when he'd been overcome by fumes and one afternoon Alfie actually passed out, so we tied a rope around his big belly and dragged him up the cellar steps to the fresh air. Health and Safety would have loved that one today.

I would often pull Alfie's leg: 'Get out of my way you silly old sod, before I throw you down your hole!' But it was Alfie who had the last laugh...

One Saturday I was making my way to a game along the rear of Fratton Park. There weren't many supporters around as there were no entrances at the back of the stadium, but I did notice a couple of chaps suddenly disappear through what appeared to be a small gate. When I got closer I saw that Alfie had neatly cut out a section of the fence to create a private turnstile and, believe it or not, was admitting punters at his very own reduced-rate ticket price. When I confronted him he simply said: 'Well, the silly old sod is not as silly as you thought he was, is he?' Alfie's secret stayed with me and I don't think anyone ever rumbled him.

Another great character on the backroom staff at Pompey

was the odd job man, George North. Now George had the filthiest mouth on any man I have ever met and he couldn't get through a simple sentence without using the big F. A typical rant would go: 'OK, you little f***ers. How the f*** are you? No f***ing about today, or I'll f*** the lot of you. Now f*** off 'cos I've got f***ing work to do.'

One morning George was given a job in the goalkeeper's loft by the Irish international Norman Uprichard, and George asked me and another apprentice to give him a hand. But with the benefit of hindsight, we should also have taken an official from the Guinness Book of World Records, to count exactly how many f-words could be spilt in half-an-hour...

George was busy in the loft when suddenly we heard a huge crash. We tiptoed up the stairs thinking the ceiling must have collapsed, but instead we were faced with the sight of George's legs thrashing in agony either side of a thick oak beam; presumably the same thick oak beam that had slammed into his wedding tackle when he slipped and fell seconds earlier. We knew it was serious but just couldn't hold our laughter when a volley of 'f***s' came firing out of George's mouth four octaves higher than we were used to.

'What the f*** has happened to my f***ing balls!' he kept squeaking. 'I can't f***ing feel them anymore!' But goodness gracious, great balls on fire; we could see them alright: they were as large as a pair of size-five footballs.

One of the directors at Pompey – a lovely man with the wonderful name of Horace Worsfold – had been appointed to keep an eye on us groundstaff boys. Without fail Horace would come and see us each morning to ask if we needed anything such as brooms, forks or gloves: you name it, he could get it. Old Horace looked at least a hundred-and-three to us youngsters, so it was no surprise when he passed away and we received an invitation to witness the scattering of his ashes.

Carefully carrying Horace in a casket, the chaplain paraded through the tunnel followed closely by the deceased's family, an array of club officials and, of course, Horace's beloved groundstaff boys. It wasn't the nicest of afternoons weather-wise, but the service proceeded calmly in the penalty box at the Fratton End; Horace's preferred spot to be sprinkled. But just as the chaplain released the old chap towards his final resting place, a gust of wind blew him halfway up the terracing. Horace had trained us boys well though, so we each fetched a broom and swept every last scrap of him back down to the pitch, just like he'd taught us.

The club's two trainers ('coaches' today) were ex-Black Watch infantryman Dougie Davidson and the aforementioned Reg Flewin, a former Royal Marine who had skippered Pompey to consecutive First Division titles in 1949 and 1950.

At first I thought the two men had a huge dislike for each other as they were always trading insults about their personal bravery and that of their respective regiments. But as I learnt the ropes I soon realised that their jibes were no more than old-fashioned banter and in fact they had huge respect and high regard for each other. Discipline, honesty and hard work were high on their training programmes and Reg, in particular, had a massive influence on the way I would approach my life. Sadly, however, my memories of them are tainted with tragedy.

I was receiving treatment one day when the sound of panic hit me: flames were licking the dressing room walls and the players and apprentices were scurrying around in desperate search of Reg, as Dougie had collapsed in the bathroom. They soon found him and although I was quickly ushered out of the way, I will never forget the tears streaming down poor Reg's face as he carried his old friend out of the dressing room in his arms. I was later told that Dougie had suffered a massive heart attack and died instantly.

Until his passing three years ago, Reg sent me a letter every Christmas and always mentioned his dear mate Dougie.

I think all footballers who've gone into the profession as an apprentice have fond memories of their first club and I have hundreds, although a few have drifted away. Thankfully though, a few years ago a friend of mine produced a booklet listing every game I played in, plus the result, ground, attendance and each player on the park.

It tells me that I made my professional debut in January 1961 aged eighteen, playing centre-half for Pompey at Roker Park in front of 36,000. We lost 4-1 and the only thing I recall about the game is that as we were about to defend a corner, one of the Sunderland players turned to me and said: 'Hey, look at that dog that's just come in, is it yours?' And yes, believe it or not, I turned around to look at that invisible mutt. Thankfully no one scored.

My second game was at home against Middlesbrough and I was asked to keep an eye on their sprightly young goal machine, Brian Howard Clough. And now that I've read that damned booklet, I'm reminded Cloughie bagged a bloody hat-trick that afternoon!

While at Portsmouth I had the honour of being picked for international duty and represented England Under-18s. I won eight caps and played in Ireland, Scotland, Portugal and Austria. And what a great side we had; I think I was the only one who didn't go on to become a real big-timer. Gordon West of Everton was in goal, John Sleeuwenhoek of Aston Villa was centre-half, Martin Peters and Terry Venables ran the midfield and Frankie Saul of Spurs, Ronnie Boyce from West Ham and Manchester City's David Wagstaffe played up front. It was a great experience to be on the park with such fine players.

Regardless, in April 1961, a revolutionary named George Smith strode into Portsmouth. Although most clubs at the time were carrying forty or fifty players feeding three teams and a youth set-up, George's plan was to work with one squad of just eighteen, which meant that thirty men were shown the door at Fratton Park.

And yours truly was one of them.

4

Hagan the Horrible

SEVERAL teams were interested in my signature when I was put on the market by Portsmouth, but as they were the closest to home, I found myself off to Queens Park Rangers. Their boss at the time, Alec Stock, had recently returned to Britain from managing AS Roma and he was nurturing a decent, mid-table Third Division outfit which harboured lofty ambitions.

Alec hired a fantastic coach from Tottenham Hotspur called Jimmy Andrews, an exponent of the great Spurs' tradition of pass-and-move. All week Jimmy would preach his sermon of 'total football', telling us to ignore what Alec said and to pass, pass and pass again. Now that's a great philosophy until you're in a competitive match and under a bit of pressure, so loud and clear from the bench Alec could often be heard screaming: 'F*** the passing! Smash it to the front men and let them sort it out!' I learnt early in my career that there can only be one boss.

Alex Stock was a clever manager – well-educated and sharp – but also thoroughly eccentric. We weren't doing too well one afternoon so at half-time he asked the players to kneel down, hold hands and pray for a bit of guidance from upstairs. I can still remember his exact words: *'Dear Lord, please forgive these young men as not one of them knows what they are doing. Guide them in the right direction. Amen.'*

I loved it at QPR: I played every week and soon built a good reputation as a strong, ball-winning defender. I was put under the wing of the club's star, Mark Lazarus, a naturally-gifted winger who was stronger than an RSJ.

I remember cruising five or six nil at home to Halifax one week, when for some stupid reason their left back kicked Mark ten feet up in the air. All hell broke loose and boots and fists were flying all over the place. The fight settled down but as the stewards were escorting the offending player from the park, a short, robust woman burst onto the pitch and began smashing everyone in sight – including a now pissed-off me – with her bright red umbrella. We later realised it was Mark's mum, who certainly wasn't going to let anyone mess with *her* little boy.

Notwithstanding irate players' mothers armed with brollies, Rangers was a friendly club. But not everyone enjoyed a joke: we had one chap named Mike Bottoms and another called Arthur Longbottom, and they took so much stick between them, they both changed their surname by deed poll. Some people just have no sense of humour.

I had been engaged to Jill since I was at Pompey and we'd been talking about getting married, seeing as I was playing so well. But before getting hitched I decided to buy my first car – a Vauxhall 10 – which has always been easy to remember as I paid the grand total of £10 for it. And what a gem it was. It only had three forward gears and the indicator arrows were operated from the top of the steering column, but Jill and I had great fun in that car and although I didn't pass my test until a year later, my provisional licence didn't affect my driving skills too much.

Both Mark Lazurus and I were getting lots of positive press for our performances so it was no surprise when Wolves made an offer for him. But just as Mark's move to the Midlands seemed set, the deal was put on hold by a freak accident.

We were pounding the track at Loftus Road (just for a change) when Mark, who was carrying on like a pork chop as usual, kicked a young groundstaff boy called Billy Smith hard up the backside. Mark just carried on running and was about fifty or sixty yards away when Billy picked up the metal plate that was used to flag up the half-time scores. He lobbed it at Mark with all his might and it locked onto its target with missile-like accuracy, smacking into the forehead of the club's naturally-gifted winger and opening a six-inch gash across his eye. Mark spent the night in hospital and the transfer had to be postponed. Billy Smith? I think he's still getting a bollocking to this day.

Incidentally, after retiring from football, Mark went on to become a minder for snooker star Steve Davis and was in his camp during the classic World Championship final against Dennis Taylor in 1985.

With Rangers riding high and second only to Northampton in the season of 1962/1963, things were looking good. Until we played at their place, that is: a huge fight kicked off and for the first time I found myself in the thick of a pitch invasion. And believe it or not, being surrounded by three or four thousand hot-blooded supporters is pretty darn scary.

By the time of the return leg the following year, Rangers were temporarily playing at White City, where many of the great international athletic meetings had been held. The security for the game was immense but even so six or seven fans from both sides still managed to scale the fence, cross the dog and running track and leg it on to the pitch faster than the police and the stewards. Mind you, they soon had the Barry White kicked out of them by twenty two fit young footballers looking for a bit of payback.

Although Rangers were going well in the league the club was strapped for cash, so the Lazurus transfer came as a big relief to the management. But when another bid came in from the Midlands – this time for me – they must have thought it was their lucky month.

I was earning £18 a week at Loftus Road, plus £2 per appearance and a £2 win bonus, so talk of a transfer was a chance to negotiate a bit extra. As such, in September 1964, I signed for First Division West Bromwich Albion, having agreed a basic wage of £27.50, plus £10 for appearances, £20 for a win and £10 for a draw.

The transfer fee went to the club at the time and the player only received what was termed an 'accrued share of benefit' from the team they were leaving. That came to £150 a year so I was also due a further £300 from QPR. They welched on the deal though and I never saw the money. Even so, I still think they were an excellent club.

Jill and I had got married on 8 June, 1963 at Molesey Methodist Church and many of the Rangers lads came along. The newlyweds were lent Bobby Robson's old club house and I ditched the Vauxhall and invested in a Hillman Minx. Then, eleven months later, Jill gave birth to a son, Nicholas. I could see the big time looming; bring it on!

Yet success in the top flight with West Brom was frustratingly out of my grasp: I spent a whole season playing in the reserves and although I was training each day with household names, I was not really progressing. All players know their standard and I knew deep down that this level was a bit too good for me. I was enjoying life with my lovely wife and young son but found looking forward a sobering experience and despite my increased basic wage, we were struggling to make ends meet.

Around this time Jill and I made friends with a smashing Baggies' fan named Ernie Hart. He always came across as a very generous and wealthy man and among the various businesses he owned was a cafe situated right next to Villa Park (which, amusingly, he only allowed Albion players to use).

One day Ernie asked if we needed any furniture so I optimistically gave him a wish-list which included beds, wardrobes, a three-piece suite, carpets and a television. The very next day Ernie turned up at our house in a large lorry crammed with all the furniture any young family could want.

'Can't have Albion players struggling,' he smiled, 'here's a small gift, with no payment necessary.'

Anyway, Jill and I were just snuggling up on our new sofa in front of our new TV thinking what a lovely chap Ernie was, when he pitched up and said he needed all the stuff back immediately or the owners of the warehouse from where it was stolen were planning to prosecute. Ah, so that's what Ernie did; he recovered stolen property. He remained a good friend but never offered us any goods again.

The centre-half for whom I understudied at The Hawthorns was Stan Jones who, luckily for him, never got injured in the two years I spent at the club. He did fall foul of a stomach bug one Saturday however, and I played well in a 2-2 draw against Nottingham Forest. But guess who played the next match? Football, as someone once said, is a funny old game and you do need a stroke of luck at times.

One lad who found fortune at West Brom was Jeff 'The King' Astle, who signed from Notts County on the same day as me. Jeff didn't give a hoot if he played or not as he really fancied himself as a singer, but the Baggies' manager at the time – a loathsome git named Jimmy Hagan – had other ideas and bullied Jeff into taking the game seriously. Hagan even banned him from singing *Fly Me To The Moon* and other popular standards while running at the opposition's defence (yep, Jeff really did do that).

It pains me to say it but credit where credit's due, Hagan

managed to turn a wannabe crooner into an international centre forward. He also got results: after his time at The Hawthorns he went to Benfica and they won every single league game under him. Mind you, he was still sacked because nobody could stand him.

I have to put on record that Jimmy Hagan is the most vicious, self-centred bastard I have ever come across. He upset so many people and I believe the Official Record Books state that West Brom is the only English football club ever to be threatened with strike action by its players (in the biting winter of 1963, Hagan refused them permission to wear tracksuit bottoms while training). But that man's most glorious display of gittery came one morning at our Spring Road training ground.

Wanting to hurry back to the stadium for some reason, Hagan ended the session early. Forgetting that the gears on his new car were in the opposite position from his old one, he jammed the vehicle into reverse instead of first and shot out of gate, smashed through the perimeter fence and tumbled down the embankment into the canal below.

A group of us rushed to the sinking car, where we found Hagan crawling through the window covered in blood. We hauled him to safety and ferried him up the steep bank to the waiting ambulance. Hagan, who could see us puffing and panting following our not inconsiderable efforts to save his skin, was naturally very grateful.

'The trouble with you lot,' he said, 'is that you ain't fit. Now piss off and get the team sheet up.'

5

The Worst Keeper
in the Third Division

WITH my football not really improving at Albion, the writing was on the wall. Indeed, one miserable morning in March 1965, Hagan pulled me into his office and in his usual charming manner told me that I was not going to make it as a top professional and perhaps it would be best for everyone if I moved on. Oh, and by the way, Mansfield Town had offered £10,000 for me and he had bitten their arm off.

'Mansfield who?' I enquired. Deep down, I still had ambitions as a player and didn't want to drop back down to the Third Division. Yet little did I know I was about to meet the greatest bunch of characters I would ever come across.

It was Tommy Eason, Mansfield's chairman, who convinced me to sign for The Stags. He picked me up from the station in his gleaming silver Bentley and the first thing I noticed was that despite being perched on a booster seat, he could still barely see over the steering wheel.

Tommy was a tiny man, certainly, but instantly likeable. He appeared to own just about everything in Mansfield and with great pride and joy he drove me to the jewel in his crown: a pig farm. But this was no common or garden pig farm, it was the most advanced in Europe and Tommy had just shelled out a couple of million pounds refurbishing it.

As we walked up and down the rows of potential gammon steaks, Tommy explained that Mansfield were struggling so he planned to buy four new players to keep them in the Third Division that season then have a shot at promotion the following year. 'How much would you want?' he asked. I told him I'd be happy to sign for the same as I was getting at Albion, plus a two-year-contract and, with my tongue in my cheek, a £2,000 cash signing-on fee. 'You've got it,' he said without hesitating. I knew I should have asked for £3,000. And perhaps a side of bacon.

In the mid-Sixties, three grand could land you a four-bedroomed house in Nottinghamshire and Jill and I thought hard about whether to buy our first home in Mansfield. We decided against it in the end as we had always planned to return to Surrey or the surrounding counties, but nevertheless we settled into a lovely house in Big Barn Lane and, much to our delight, Jill gave birth at Kings Mill Hospital on 4 July 1966 to our second child; a beautiful little girl named Claire.

Over at Mill Field, Tommy Eason's four-player injection kept the team in the Third Division as planned and he had also attracted a new manager, Tommy Cummings (who later went to Villa). Cummings simply topped up the nucleus of a good side with a handful of quality players who were available on free transfers: former Newcastle stars Dave Hollins, Tommy Knox, Bill McKinney and Bill Curry; ex-Liverpool defender Phil Ferns and left-back Billy Richardson from Sunderland. Whatever, the signings had one thing in common; they were all absolute plant pots.

Bill McKinney, for instance, played more than four hundred league games for Newcastle but he never trained a day at Mansfield and would stretch out on the treatment table all week until making a miraculous recovery each Friday morning. How the manager put up with the skiving I will never know, but Cummings once admitted to me that his lax approach was because he knew the players would always give one hundred per cent on the park on a Saturday afternoon. Even so, the team did get away with all kinds of horseplay.

Faced with training one bitter morning, we literally locked ourselves in the dressing room and tucked ourselves up with mugs of tea and a deck of cards. Regular threats from the trainers fell on deaf ears so up piped the boss: 'Now come on lads, let's be fair; you know you've got to train,' Tommy pleaded through the keyhole.

'Piss off, it's too cold.'

'Lads, please.'

'Piss off.'

The stand-off lasted an hour or so, until we eventually unlocked the door and a meeting was called. It went something like this:

PLAYERS: You know how cold it is boss; we really can't train.

TOMMY: I say you've got to train.

PLAYERS: We say we're not training.

TOMMY: I'll stop your money, then you'll know who calls the shots around here.

PLAYERS: If we train today and if you even think about stopping our money, we won't have a go for you on Saturday.

TOMMY: Well, if you promise to have a go on Saturday, there'll be no training today and no money stopped – agreed?

And they talk about player-power today.

Tommy Eason's splash of cash reaped rewards at Mill Field but his show of wealth was not confined to the pitch: every six months or so he would trade in both his Bentley and his Riley for new ones, with the irony totally lost on him that while the quality of his cars was 'high', the standard of his driving was 'atrocious'.

The problem I had was that Tommy always wanted me – the team skipper – to travel to away matches with him, which was always a trial and often a tribulation.

I won't forget schlepping home in the early hours from a mid-week game somewhere miles away. I was snoozing in the front and one of the club directors and the local chief of police were asleep in the back. Suddenly we were jolted awake by an almighty smash: an almighty smash soon diagnosed as Tommy using his brand new Bentley to rip a pair of metal bollards out of the ground and wedge them deep beneath the bonnet.

I hadn't counted how many cans of Top Deck Tommy had sunk that night, but the rest of us were well tanked up. Nevertheless, the chief of police sobered up quickly enough and in a flash, two squad cars were having their boots loaded with bits of broken Bentley and what remained of the bollards. They were then driven to Tommy's farm where, in a distant corner, the debris – or 'evidence', as some would call it – was buried. Meanwhile, Tommy's transport firm hooked up the Bentley and Her Majesty's Police Force chauffeured everyone down to Tommy's hotel for sausage, egg and chips. Overnight, the Bentley was fully repaired and re-sprayed and the following afternoon was gift-wrapped to Tommy. Owning half a town certainly has its perks.

Looking back I also recall a very merry Christmas Eve spent with the Mansfield lads. Following a short training session, after which we'd each been given a bottle of whisky and an unplucked turkey with its head still on as a Christmas box, we decamped to the pub. When we fell out of it around half-four in the afternoon, our little winger, Stuart Brace, thought it would be a good idea to invite some of us back to his place for a few more drinks and a singsong.

Waiting arms folded on the doorstep was Audrey, Stuart's

wife. She stood at least six inches taller than him and was rather miffed with her husband as he had apparently promised to be home by midday to take the family shopping and then on to the cinema. Regardless, we all bundled into the house and began filling ourselves with more yuletide cheer.

About to break into a messy version of *The Twelve Days of Christmas*, we were stopped in our tracks by Audrey, who launched into Stuart with the mother of all mouthfuls and, whipping up a greasy storm of feathers and giblets, began clubbing her errant husband around the head with the nearest turkey to hand. Well, sozzled as we were, we sobered up within seconds and ducking for cover we scarpered, bellowing with laughter at the glad tidings of great joy in the Brace household that Christmas.

When we faced near-neighbours Sheffield Wednesday in the Fourth Round of the FA Cup in February 1967, the whole of Mansfield was keyed up and a crowd of 50,000 was expected at Hillsborough. To prepare, Tommy Cummings announced that he was taking the team away on a special training programme to – wait for it – Skegness. Naturally, we packed our golf clubs and drinking mugs and did just one day's training. The match? Well, we were 1-0 down with fifteen minutes to go and lost 4-0. Tommy just said: 'I think we should have trained for at least three days.'

Funnily enough, it was in that cup-tie that I heard for the first time a wisecrack that has often been repeated: following a crunching tackle by Phil Ferns that laid Wednesday winger Johnny Fantham out cold, everyone was calling for a stretcher.

'F*** the stretcher,' bawled Phil in his thick Scouse, 'bring a blanket; I think he's dead!'

The pair of goalkeepers at Mansfield Town, Colin Treharne from the reserves and first team regular Dave Hollins – the brother of ex-England international John and uncle of TV sports presenter Chris – were also good entertainment value.

I remember being 5-1 up at home to Peterborough one Saturday when a peal of laughter swept around the ground. At first the players couldn't work out what was going on, but then we noticed that Dave, who had hardly been rushed off his feet that afternoon, had sat down against one of the uprights, pulled his cap down over his eyes and gone to sleep. A local photographer took a snap of him and the story made the national press: the manager and chairman were far from impressed but Dave swore blind that he was just kidding, not kipping. Well, that's what he reckoned.

As for Colin, he was a very poor back-up to Dave and played only occasionally. But I do recall one game he started, before which the players sneakily made up a sign in the dressing room and fixed it to the back of his jersey.

To the usual gentle applause, we jogged out of the tunnel to the home end and began warming up. But as Colin turned around to face a few practice shots, the crowd behind the goal exploded when they read on his back: *I'm the Worst Keeper in the Third Division!* That was hilarious in itself, but the thing that particularly tickled me was Colin later maintained that the crowd was giving him a cheer, when actually they were shouting: 'Too bloody true!'

I can't see players getting away with that kind of monkey business today. Whatever, the fun I was enjoying at Mansfield ended with a jolt when I badly twisted a knee and had to have my cartilage removed. Two months later I had lost my place and in September 1967, Mansfield sold me to Gillingham Football Club for £7,500. Jill was happy with the idea as it meant moving nearer home and I was quite keen as the boss at Priestfield at the time was Basil Hayward, a former Portsmouth player whose boots I cleaned as an apprentice.

So off to Kent we went.

6

Golf Balls and Knuckle Dusters

THE contrast between what I was used to at Mansfield and what I found when I arrived at Gillingham was immense.

Mansfield had been fielding an aging squad and as you've read, the players were so laid-back they were often found horizontal in the dressing room with a copy of the *Racing Post* on their face. Although the lads at Gillingham were not nearly as much fun, they were considerably younger and far more disciplined, which served to remind me that it was perhaps time to stop larking about and focus on being a serious professional once again.

Arriving in Kent the Williams' family moved into a decent club house in Rainham, which backed onto a cricket field. Sometimes, an elderly chap who looked like a tramp would come to the back gate for a natter: he was a very pleasant fellow and always wore the same scruffy old mac and battered cap. As the months passed I learnt his name was Sid Galloway and he was a huge Gills' supporter. He'd been a farmer all his life but had made millions when the Government made a compulsory purchase order to build the M2 across his land four years earlier in 1963. I remember him telling me that he'd never had electricity at the farm where he lived with his wife and brother, so after the cash windfall from the Government fell into his lap, the first thing Sid did was have electricity installed. The second thing Sid did was to buy seven television sets; one for each room, including the bathroom. As they say, you should never judge a book by its tatty cover.

The family settled happily in the Medway Towns and I was pleased to be playing regular first team football again. Basil Hayward made me skipper as soon as I arrived and to be honest I have always enjoyed the responsibility of being in charge. Even so, there was much work to be done at Gillingham if we were to build a good team playing with a winning spirit.

When we weren't training I spent my spare time improving my golf and one afternoon Gordon Riddick, our big centre forward who we'd just bought from Luton Town, came to the house to show off his brand new driver. 'Let's take it out on the cricket field and hit a few balls,' he suggested.

Well, after a couple of swings, Gordon caught one as sweet as you like and the ball sailed towards the cluster of new houses that had recently been built on the far side of the field.

'It's not going to, is it?' I hoped.

'No, I don't think so,' said Gordon, a second or so before we heard a horrifying smash in the distance.

I doubt you'll ever see two blokes leg it as fast as we did but being good boys at heart, guilt got the better of us and we knocked on every door in the area hoping to apologise. Oddly, no one reported any breakages so to this day it's a complete mystery where that golf ball landed. For the record though, if, in the winter of 1967, you'd just bought a lovely new house in Rainham which backed onto a lovely cricket field and you had your lovely new greenhouse shattered one afternoon by a wayward Slazenger 7: it was Gordon Riddick, not me.

During the many months I was (not) playing at West Brom, I was given a great deal of advice by Aston Villa's Phil Woosnam, the Welsh inside-right (and cousin to golfer Ian) who won seventeen caps for his country and eventually became the Commissioner of the North American Soccer League. Phil got me interested in the coaching side of the game and encouraged me to go to Lilleshall to get myself qualified.

In my first managerial role I had taken The Royal George – a pub team filled with part-time pros from the Birmingham area – to the final of the Sunday League Cup. It was a good side and we certainly had fun: Sunday lunchtimes in the pub often included a 'Gentlemen Only' show, which was designed to help the players raise their money (and other things).

Although we lost the final we arranged a trip to Manchester as a slap on the back for everyone. We hired two coaches and the players, supporters and management squeezed themselves in among the local colliery workers.

And what a great day out we had. It kicked off with the
1967 Charity Shield final between Manchester United and
Tottenham Hotspur, the 3-3 draw in which Pat Jennings left
Alex Stepney floundering when he scored arguably the most
famous goal by a keeper. After the match at Old Trafford we
pit-stopped at Belle Vue stadium to watch the motorcycling,
before enjoying a dance at Mecca and a late Chinese. We
eventually rolled home at five in the morning.

As I now held a full coaching badge, one of the Gillingham
squad asked if I was interested in teaching sport at Inner
London schools. I welcomed the idea and will never forget
the months I spent in Sydenham in the London Borough of
Lewisham.

I hadn't been there five minutes when I realised that my
coaching knowledge was likely to be rendered redundant and
my man-management skills pushed to the limit: in the first
week alone I confiscated two flick knives and a knuckle duster.

One day we were doing athletics – long jump to be precise –
when a local herbert named Joey Smales pitched up on the track
dressed in jeans and bovver boots. Joey had been excluded from
the school for bad behaviour and was clearly there to disrupt
the session. He chose the wrong day though and I wasn't in the
mood to be messed around, so I simply picked him up, carried
him to the dressing room and, quite literally, hung him up on a
coat hook. Joey failed to see the funny side and as I headed for
the school gates later that afternoon, there he was, larging it up
alongside his elder brothers.

'Here it comes,' I thought, and began to brace myself

for a few blows when, to my surprise, one of the brothers announced that Joey was actually there to apologise. 'It's about time someone hung him up,' he said, 'he's been getting far too big for his boots.'

Believe it or not, several years later I bumped into Joey and, fully expecting him to say he'd just been released from Parkhurst, I asked him what he'd been up to. 'I'm a ladies hairdresser, and doing very well,' he said. I nearly fainted.

During the early part of the 1969/1970 season Gillingham were going great guns and embarked on a record-breaking FA Cup run, which led us to a Fifth Round tie away at Watford. There was huge respect for the Cup back in the Sixties and Seventies so it was a major achievement for Gillingham to get so far. The media coverage was rife and everyone at the club was looking forward to the big day.

In the build-up to the match Britain endured a fortnight of torrential rain and a number of games were called off – in those days the weather had to be horrendous for a match to be postponed. Ours wasn't though and we played Watford on a Vicarage Road pitch that was caked in mud. The game was an absolute farce and we lost 2-1 thanks to their centre forward's winner, which he scored by simply beating our keeper in a race when the ball got stuck in the sludge. It was no way to go out of the Fifth Round and although the papers said we were unlucky and that the game should never have been played, they never print that next to the result, do they?

After the cup defeat the team slid down the table and

only just managed to avoid relegation. That did happen the following season though, and Basil Hayward was sacked.

Gillingham's chairman at the time was Dr Clifford Grossmark, a well-respected businessman who had prudently kept the club in the black for years. But there was dissent coming from the terraces so he swiped Andy Nelson from Charlton Athletic and gave him cash to spend on the team. I liked Dr Grossmark and I really liked playing for Gillingham, but I think the new manager was looking for a younger centre-half and my days appeared to be numbered.

Nevertheless, coaching was now playing an increasingly large part in my life and at Gillingham I set up a youth section named The Gillettes. Although none of the kids were old enough to even think about bum fluff let alone grow it, believe it or not the club attracted sponsorship from Gillette razors. Dozens of youngsters would turn up for a game each week so we branched out into organised teams and it was the first time I learnt how to get everyone singing from the same hymn sheet.

However, no sooner had we launched the youth group a headline on the back page of the local sports paper screamed: *GILLS TEAM OF SHAME*. At first I wondered what on Earth someone from the first team had been up to, but the chairman and manager called me in and as head of the youth section, I was read the riot act.

Apparently, during an Under-8's tie against Sheerness, two of the dads had got into a scuffle. From that day on I always insisted that parents sign waiver forms and that all press stories must go through a professional communications man, which has since saved me hours and hours of aggro.

After five seasons at Gillingham I was due for a benefit year. Instead, I was simply thanked for all that I had done and told to clear my locker. There is no sentiment in football – which I understand – but surely sometimes clubs don't have to be quite so severe.

I had seen it coming though, so had already put out a few feelers: I was really looking for a player/manager job but they were (and still are) not very easy to find. I did receive a couple of good offers to play semi-professionally but in the end they came to nothing. Then the manager of Crystal Palace, Bert Head, phoned to say there was a team in the South African city of Durban who were looking for a centre-half to play for three months. I told Bert I was interested.

Around the same time I was contacted by the young chairman at Maidstone United, who asked me to consider playing for them. That was the first time I met Jim Thompson, and so began a relationship that would last for many years. Jim talked me into doing a 'real job' as he put it, so in the autumn of 1972 I signed as both a Stones' player and their representative for the Kent Evening Post, with the proviso that I would be free to play in South Africa should the opportunity arise.

When I wandered down Leafy Lane for the first time, Maidstone had just appointed a new manager, the former Gillingham legend Ernie Morgan. At Priestfield Ernie had scored the highest number of goals in a single season – thirty-one in 1954/1955 – a record which still stands to this day (he shares it with Brian Yeo).

Ernie had replaced the management pairing of Bobby Houghton and the current England boss Roy Hodgson. Their sacking had been rather controversial, as they had taken The Stones on their debut as a semi-pro outfit in the Southern League Division One South to within a point of the joint leaders Waterlooville and Ramsgate. Not that that carried much truck with Mr Thompson.

Bobby and Roy went on to become very successful professional managers of course, and spent a great deal of time working together. Bobby's moment of glory came in 1979 when he took Swedish side Malmo to the final of the European Cup (which they lost 1-0 to Nottingham Forest). It's a shame he didn't stay with The Stones because perhaps he could have taken us to those same dizzy heights.

Both Bobby and Roy spent a lot of time playing and working in South Africa and while they were at Berea Park FC in Pretoria I can remember Roy being in the side that my Durban United team thumped 6-0. Bobby married a South African girl and I had little contact with the pair over the next forty years: I sat next to Bobby on a flight back from South Africa in 1974 and I had a brief conversation with Roy when I was negotiating Chris Smalling's move to Fulham in 2008. But our paths did cross on one more occasion...

Under Roy's management Fulham were sponsored by the electrical giant LG and Mark Hill, our old left back at

Maidstone, was the executive liaison representative between the company and the club. Coincidentally, just prior to the Christmas of 2009, Roy had ordered a twenty-inch television from Mark for his wife to watch in the kitchen and I had bought a similar model as a present for my granddaughter, although I had been under strict instructions to ensure that hers must come with a rather natty pink edging. Anyway, you can probably tell where this story is heading and sure enough, during delivery the two sets got mixed up so after a quick conversation, Roy pulled Chris Smalling to one side and told him to adopt a pivotal holding role – as Santa's big helper – and I met Chris on a very cold Christmas Eve in Maidstone to exchange televisions. To this day my granddaughter still has the England manager's old TV set fixed to her bedroom wall.

Maidstone have had some excellent coaches over the years and apart from Peter Taylor and John Still, there have been none better than Bobby Houghton and Roy Hodgson. We really should have given one of those four a ten-year deal and taken our chances. Hindsight is a wonderful tool. Whatever, I have digressed.

When I arrived at Maidstone in 1972, Ernie Morgan hit me with a bombshell by informing me that although I had played three hundred games as a right back or, preferably, as a centre-half, he wanted me to embark on a career as a midfielder. 'It'll be a doddle for you,' he reckoned.

I can still remember one of my first games in the new position: an evening match away at Trowbridge. It had been raining all day and the game was lucky to be on. We had only been playing on the Wiltshire mud for a few minutes when I was faced with a good old-fashioned fifty-fifty tackle. 'Right up my street,' I thought to myself, but as I went crashing in with the opposition player the pain that shot up my leg and into the area where my mother would never have kissed me was immense. I had tramlines of stud marks from the open sock on my ankle leading right up into the realms of my family jewels. It was without doubt the worst tackle I had ever encountered and as I sat in agony on the four-hour coach ride home, I thanked Ernie several times for changing my position.

Like many men named Ernie – think comedian Ernie Wise, lifelong Stones' fan Ernie Munn, Ernie from *Sesame Street* and Ernie the reckless-driving milkman friend of Benny Hill – Ernie Morgan was a first-class character and always up for a laugh. The only problem was that someone, somewhere, for some reason, had told him he could sing. He wasn't *that* bad, but he was certainly no Frank Sinatra (or, for that matter, even a Jeff Astle). If the team won Ernie would insist on crooning to both the players and the supporters and I'm sure he sang to his family at home and probably to the customers on his window cleaning round as well.

Even as recently as last year, not long before his sad death at the age of eighty-six, I attended a reunion of Gillingham players and as Ernie got up to receive an award, he grabbed the microphone: 'Thank you very much for this honour,' he said. 'But before I go, I'd like to give you a little rendition of...' and off he went again.

Although Maidstone had won the Southern League Division One South by the February of 1973, Jim either sacked Ernie or he left (rumour has it he slunk off warbling a version of *Show Me The Way To Go Home*).

February was also the start of the football season in South Africa and Bert Head called again to check if I still fancied playing in Durban. Jim tried to persuade me to stay with Maidstone but with the Southern League title already in the bag, I relished the opportunity to experience a different way of life and test my footballing nous on another continent.

I had been tempted by South Africa several years earlier when I was playing at QPR: I was often driven to Loftus Road by Stuart Leary, a South African who not only played centre forward for Charlton Athletic before coming to Rangers but also opened the batting for Kent. He talked a lot about South Africa so I was already interested in seeing the country before Bert Head suggested the move.

It was very difficult leaving Jill, Nick and Claire at home for three months, but as a family we agreed that the experience could lead the family on an exciting adventure...

7

Gateway to South Africa

IN 1973 the city of Durban supported three football teams and, believe it or not, I wasn't sure which one I would be turning out for.

The major side in town was the aptly-named Durban City, who were drawing gates of up to 20,000. Durban United attracted around 8,000 fans while Durban Celtic – a youth set-up which had splintered from United – had about a thousand supporters. And yes, you've guessed it, my team turned out to be Durban Celtic; bottom of the league with three points.

At the time there were four national leagues as apartheid was still very much in place. That meant a Black league, a Coloured league, an Indian league and a White league so my powers of deduction soon told me which one I would be playing in. Living with apartheid felt very awkward at first but I slowly grew accustomed to it. In addition to the country's politics I also had to adjust to the weather. I would run in the sun for an hour-and-a-half each day and also train three evenings a week. Matches were played at four o'clock on Sunday afternoons and there was an occasional night game.

Celtic was run by a group of very wealthy bookmakers and car dealers; all great blokes who could choke a horse with the cash in their pockets. But while the team was a mixture of young men and even younger men who were very fit and occasionally talented, they had been badly coached and were highly disorganised.

I clearly remember my first two games – we were beaten 5-0 at home by Durban City and then 7-1 away at Cape Town Spurs. In need of some support the manager asked if I would help him pull the side together and as I wasn't doing much else, I agreed to assist him in the half-a-dozen games left before I was due to fly home.

We immediately played nine behind the ball and one up. As it turned out the team had four exceptional players: a centre forward called Ian Bender (who would eventually become the national side's number nine), a tall, elegant midfielder named Neil Roberts (who I later took to the States with me) and two absolute flying machines; one at home on the right and one naturally left-sided. The right winger was Mervyn Hauptfleisch and years later I watched him win the 200 metre dash at the national competition in Windheok. My word he was quick.

The change in the team formation and a fat slice of good fortune saw us win five of the remaining seven fixtures and Celtic move into a safe position. This was my first taste of management (apart from The Royal George pub side of course) and I had plenty of time to mull over my experiences on the eleven hour flight home.

Back in Britain there were no offers on the table that appealed to me: plenty of non-league teams wanted me to play for them but there were no management jobs. However, I soon received a call from Celtic in Durban who wanted to send one of their directors over to offer me the dual job of both playing for and managing the side.

The day Peter Balfour arrived from South Africa is an easy one to recall. He came to our house in Rainham to discuss terms but no one spoke for three hours as we sat watching television. No, we didn't settle down for back-to-back episodes of *Upstairs Downstairs* but were riveted to a live recording of man's first landing on the Moon. Television had not yet been launched in South Africa so Peter sat glued to the screen as Neil Armstrong took his giant leap for mankind. Anyway, just as the Stars and Stripes was being planted, a counter offer for my services was made by the second-largest team in Durban: United. The club's owner Cyril Murley was in London and wanted to meet so in twenty-four hours, I had two offers to consider and a massive decision to make – which offer to take or stay in Britain and take my chances.

The deal from Celtic was good and of course I knew the people, but United's offer was even better and they were a bigger club so as upsetting as it was, I told the kids at Celtic that I was going to their bitter enemy.

Cyril Murley was a self-made Rand billionaire and is without shadow of a doubt the wealthiest man I have ever met. His hobby was collecting gold and diamonds and he owned property all over South Africa. Also in his portfolio was the country's biggest chain of drive-in cinemas, which was mega business with television not yet up and running.

Jill and I made the difficult decision to leave home and those who've done likewise will know what upset it can cause your parents. Of course we didn't make the choice lightly but it was the first chance I had been given to get into football management which was what I wanted to do. At the end of the day the family were happy to embrace the opportunity so off we set on the journey of a lifetime.

It took us a while to settle into our new life: living in hotel rooms was far from ideal – particularly for eight-year-old Nick and six-year-old Claire – but we eventually found a suitable house to buy and things began to look brighter.

Cyril Murley told me he wanted United to become the top team in town and was prepared to pay for it. Before my arrival he'd thrown a lot of money at the side and most of his players were mainly has-beens from the English and Scottish leagues. I wasn't going to turn down the chance to bring over a few seasoned pros of course, so off I popped back to Britain with Cyril and his cheque book to buy a few players.

In the five we brought back was the Rangers and Scotland centre-half Ronnie McKinnon. And despite him being thirty-nine and on his last legs, I also nabbed Johnny Haynes from local rivals City: he could still pass a good ball. Another signing was a full-back from Clyde called Eddie Mulheron, who was a great bloke but something of a heavy-drinking loose cannon.

Eddie was the first player I ever had a stand-up fight with, which came about as the result of me bringing to his attention the rotten way he treated his wife and family. We were in a bar and he picked me up and threw me across a table, which took a bit of doing as I was weighing in at around fourteen stones by then. He later apologised for his behaviour but eventually learnt the harshest lesson of all: in another fit of temper he clumped a referee and got banned from football for life. It was a great shame as he was a very good player.

I also brought Jackie Sinclair over from Leicester City and he was the reason I became known throughout my career in South Africa by the nickname 'Iron Man'...

We were playing a local derby and I called Jackie off near the end. As he was crossing the touchline, he took off his sweaty shirt and threw it in my face. Like Sinclair, my assistant at the time, Craig Watson, was a Scot. 'You'd better have a word about that boss,' suggested Craig, so I followed Jackie up the tunnel.

By the time I reached the dressing rooms, Jackie was just getting into the shower. I told him to get his arse out of it straight away but as he turned, he caught his eye on the shower head and from the tiniest nick the jetting water sent blood streaming down his face and body, forming a claret river around his feet.

The game finished and as the players drifted back to the dressing room, everyone became convinced that I'd given

Portrait of a young footballer, in my days
with Portsmouth.

The very smart Esher Primary School First XI, 1953.
I'm in the front row, second from the left.

The slightly scruffy Molesey FC Under 18s, 1957.
I'm second from the right in the back row, aged 15.

PORTSMOUTH FOOTBALL COMPANY, LIMITED.

Fratton Park, Portsmouth.   Phone: 31204

Manager:
F. COX

F.A. Cup Finalists 1928-29 and 1933-34
F.A. Cup Winners 1938-39
London (War) Cup Finalists 1941-42
Football League Division 1 Championship
1948-49 and 1949-50

President:
FIELD MARSHAL
THE VISCOUNT
MONTGOMERY
OF ALAMEIN
K.G., G.C.B., D.S.O.

Secretary:
R. W. MULCOCK

12th February, 1960.

Mr. & Mrs. Williams,
19 Douglas Road,
ESHER, Surrey.

Dear Mr. & Mrs. Williams,

I thought I would drop you a line
upon Bill's selection to play for
England against Scotland.

Naturally you are very proud, as
we are at Fratton Park, that Bill should
receive International recognition.   It
is an honour well deserved, because
throughout the Season he has worked
extremely hard at his training.

I hope this is a fore-runner of a
long and successful career in football.

I should like to add that Bill's
general character and personality will
be a wonderful asset to any Club and
Dressing Room spirit.

Yours sincerely,

Roy Lewin

Assistant Manager.

My postbag is not so exciting these days.

THE FOOTBALL ASSOCIATION.

PATRON:
HER MAJESTY THE QUEEN.
PRESIDENT:
H.R.H. THE DUKE OF GLOUCESTER, K.G., K.T.

SECRETARY:
SIR STANLEY ROUS, C.B.E., J.P.

TELEGRAPHIC ADDRESS:
"FOOTBALL ASSOCIATION
PADD. LONDON."

Any reply to this letter should be
addressed to The Secretary and
the following reference quoted.

22, LANCASTER GATE,
LONDON. W.2.

21st March 1960

WRO

D. Williams Esq.

Dear Sir,

Youth International Match
England v. East Germany

I have pleasure in informing you that you have been
selected to play for England in the above match, on the
ground of Portsmouth FC., on Saturday 2nd April 1960., kick-
off at 3 p.m.

I shall be pleased to hear, by return of post, that
you are fit and able to do so.

An itinerary will be sent to you in due course.

Yours truly,

Stanley Rous.

Secretary

England v East Germany, Fratton Park, 1960. Many of the team went on to enjoy an illustrious career: to the right of keeper Gordon West stands Martin Peters; Owen Dawson is next to me, and second from the left in the front row is Frankie Saul, then Terry Venables, Ronnie Boyce and David Wagstaffe.

Stepping out with Jill on the sand at Southsea, 1960.

QPR's rakish new signing, 1961.

You should have seen the other guy.

Wedding belles, 1963.

Modelling for Palitoy's Striker game at West Brom ('Players have one moveable leg controlled by a rod which attaches to the head. Press the head down to propel the ball').

The Baggies' 1964/65 Spot the Bastard competition (clue: Jimmy Hagan is in the middle wearing a smooth suit and smug expression). I'm in the row behind, fourth from right.

When I returned to Loftus Road with Mansfield in February 1967, QPR's prolific striker Les Allen found himself kept in check during a goalless draw.

Gillingham jam, 1968, featuring Carl Gilbert on drums, Dennis Hunt on piano, me and Bob Moffat on guitars, and Gordon Riddick and Bill Brown on vocals. Presumably, the band who lent us the gear were called For Example, but couldn't fit their full name on the bass drum.

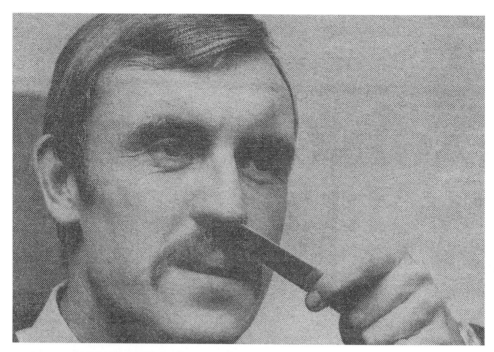

Above: *'Big Bill Williams, popular 27-year-old Gillingham defender, who has been suffering from a nagging hamstring injury for the past three weeks, has not been idling away his time while out of the game. He has been busy cultivating a Pancho moustache.'* Chatham Standard, December 1969.

Clearing the lines at Priestfield against Reading in August 1970, watched by Ray Bailey and Brian Yeo.

Jackie a jolly good pasting. No matter how many times we both denied it, the story was leaked to the press and the headline on the back of the paper the next morning was: *IRON MAN DELIVERS JUSTICE.*

At the time a good friend of mine, Ron Newman, was coaching the Ford Lauderdale Strikers, and he advised me how to handle the press conference that would inevitably follow. Ron had experienced the very same problem not long before, when Strikers' winger George Best had thrown his shirt into Ron's face. After the incident Ron had told the press pack: 'I was delighted with George's accuracy. We had spent the week practicing how he would show his disappointment at being substituted by throwing his shirt in my face, and I have to say the throw was perfect.'

Ron, as you can tell, was a funny man and told me a story about something which happened to him when he first arrived in the States involving the President of the Strikers; a very powerful man called Joe Robbie.

Joe, who also owned the Miami Dolphins. was a good guy, apparently, but a notorious boozer. Anyway, the Strikers were playing the Tampa Bay Rowdies in a play-off game and Ron and Joe were giving interviews live on CBS television. The announcer said his piece, then spoke to Ron before turning to Joe for a final word, only to find him sound asleep in his chair snoring off a few vodkas in front of half-a-million viewers.

Armed with the new signings Durban United were doing well in the league and sat just above City in the table. Each

Monday morning I would meet Cyril Murley at his office at the drive-in to discuss the upcoming matches and any strategies we had in mind.

Cyril had an Indian secretary, Abdulla, who did everything for his boss and in return was treated like a dog. I remember one day Murley phoned me in total panic asking if I'd seen hide or hair of Abdulla. I told him I hadn't but he still wanted me at the drive-in as quickly as possible. I arrived to find an ashen-looking Murley staring at the open safe in his private office.

'All the cash has gone and only me and Abdulla have a key,' he said. 'Are you sure you haven't seen him?'

I asked Cyril how much was missing. 'The lot: about one-and-a-half million Rand' (about £150,000 at the time).

I suggested he phoned the police. 'Are you mad!' he blasted. 'It's undeclared money – I'd go to jail!'

The epilogue to this tale is that two years later, I took a team to play in Johannesburg where, believe it or not, I bumped into Abdulla. 'I told you Williams that I'd get that bastard one day,' he said, then skipped away into the distance.

Despite the fact that United were steadily climbing the table, Murley wanted me to snaffle the league's leading goalscorer, Bobby Viljoen, who was regularly rippling the net for Rangers FC in Johannesburg. I therefore negotiated a fee of £26,000 and Bobby moved to Durban.

We lost every one of Bobby's first five games and he hadn't scored once, so we soon slipped into mid-table no-man's land. This was my first season in a big position in a big league and

I was learning fast. The system I was using – essentially a passing game – was one that Bobby had never played. 'I score my goals when we're defending,' he told me. 'I like to sit on the last defender and when the ball gets smashed up front I get after it.'

I took Bobby's comments on board and whenever we were defending and the opposition's back four were on the halfway line, we would drill controlled balls behind their defence and sure enough the lad would nine times out of ten create a chance. He had tremendous speed and was probably the fittest player that ever played for me.

After the change in tactics we went on a good run and my first year as a full-time manager ended with the team in fourth spot, which was a huge improvement on the previous season.

Bobby Viljoen had made a strong impact on the team but the more I grew to know him the stranger he seemed. He was not only fit but also very aggressive. Then, at the end of the season, he simply disappeared into thin air.

Several years later I hooked up with Bobby in America, when he laid bare the biggest surprise I have ever heard: not only did he reveal that he was homosexual, but that he had been working in Durban as a professional rent boy. He'd gone missing as he was suddenly shipped to the States when his life was threatened in South Africa. To this day Bobby is the only homosexual player I have met in the game. Mind you, if they all performed the way he did, I wouldn't have a problem managing an entire team of gay men. Well, that's assuming that they didn't insist on calling themselves Friends of Dorothy United.

Despite the successful season, my full-time job was about to become part-time and I needed to find another source of income. Luckily fate threw me – and someone else – a lifeline...

I was enjoying a beer at the Harbour Bar in Durban one afternoon when an old boy found himself literally all at sea when his boat capsized. A stranger sitting opposite asked if I could swim and when I told him I could, he suggested we jump quickly into his boat to fish the poor fellow out. Within half-an-hour later we had rescued the man and just like the last old codger I helped whose life was in danger – that bastard Hagan, of course – he didn't even hang around long enough to say thank you.

Anyway, the boat-owner introduced himself as Brian Deane and we went back to the bar to have a chat over another pint. I mentioned my close-season circumstances and he said he may have something for me: it turned out to be a job selling metal hospital and office furniture and as I had nothing else in the pipeline, I took him up on his offer and started straight away.

Deane's Office Furniture was a small operation: there was one other salesman, an Indian toolmaker, five Zulu labourers and Brian Deane's wife, who kept the books and acted as receptionist. We only had twenty clients but Brian's father was the managing director of the massive steel operator GKN Sankey, and he kept us afloat by giving Brian all the small jobs that he couldn't be bothered with.

I began a strict regime of starting work at six in the morning, finishing at four, then training three nights a week from eight to ten before matches on a Sunday. They were punishing hours and I didn't see enough of the family but at least we were doing better thanks to the second income.

As Cyril Murley had wanted, Durban United was now a major force in the city and our performances were attracting an additional 4,000 fans to each game. We also reached the final of the Embassy Cup – the South African equivalent of the FA Cup – against Cape Town City.

We lost 2-1 in a match that we had dominated and afterwards Cyril burst into the dressing room and gave everyone a good slagging, in particular the brothers Ian and Malcolm Filby (who I'd signed from Leyton Orient). Murley's outburst didn't sit comfortably with me though and it was just as well that the stewards ushered him away before the Iron Man could take him to task.

Talking of the Filby boys, I'll never forget the colourful day when I nipped over to East Ham to sign them. They lived in a small terraced house and the family's footballing loyalties were divided between bitter rivals West Ham and Spurs. When I pitched up the clan were sinking beer and munching sandwiches around the dining room table, peppering a monstrous row with language so foul it would have made Bernard Manning blush.

Eventually reaching the end of her tether, Mrs Filby strode out of the kitchen in her pinny and smacked her hand down on the table. 'Lads, please!' she bawled. 'You know we have an important guest with us today! So less of that f***ing language!'

It turned out that the entire family swore like sailors and when the boys were playing for United we would often bet Ian – who had the dirtiest gob of them all – that he couldn't last two minutes without swearing. He never picked up any money.

My second season in charge at Durban United ended with us taking the runner's up position: Cape Town did the double which was no surprise as they had a tremendous team. My third season started promisingly as we had strengthened the side and were looking to emulate what Cape Town had achieved the previous year.

Meanwhile, my job at Deane's was becoming very demanding and my knack for selling was bringing in more orders than we could handle. While visiting the hospitals a few of the doctors had suggested that we consider manufacturing wheelchairs, as every single one in South Africa was imported. I mentioned it to Brian who said he'd think about it once I'd gathered all the relevant information.

Well into the second half of the season with United top of the league, the unthinkable happened: we travelled to Johannesburg to play Arcadia Shepherds in the quarter-final of the Embassy Cup and I made the mistake that lost us the game. For the second time Murley burst into the dressing room spitting venom – much of it directed at me – but on this occasion there were no stewards around so the Iron Man took it upon himself to physically throw him out into the corridor. Murley later claimed that I had hit him and he sacked me on the Monday morning.

With the team doing so well he didn't really want to do it, so I agreed to take a year's money and say that the parting was by mutual consent and that there would be no further comment from either party.

Regardless, a month later the ex-West Ham and England centre forward Johnny Byrne left Durban City for Cape Town City and I was offered the top managerial job in town.

Simultaneously, Brian had worked out how to manufacture the wheelchairs and the company had been backed by the Government to the tune of ten national contracts. Overnight then, I had landed the plum football role in the city and had been promoted to General Manager at Deane's Office Furniture, now renamed Deane's Wheelchairs.

Durban City had struggled over the previous couple of seasons but not as badly as I discovered when I started my new job. The club was bankrupt and could not afford to pay their expensive overseas players so my first task was to let twelve of them go, just keeping the local born ones.

So, like you would, I immediately nipped back to United and pinched three of their exceptional South African youngsters. Celtic were on the verge of collapse at the time so I also signed national regulars Ian Bender and Neil Roberts from them. At a quick check I had five national team players and my mind was made up to go with an all-South African line-up.

I'd brought my assistant Craig Watson with me from United. Craig had grown up with Alex Ferguson and was always banging on about what a star he was going to become (that's Alex, not Craig). Anyway, years later, in 2001, Craig was a pall-bearer at the great Jim Baxter's funeral and returned from Glasgow (Jim's ashes were buried at Ibrox) with news that Alex had invited the pair of us over to his house to play a bit of golf. The weekend was eventually arranged between Craig and Alex and I, but a few months before the trip Craig became very ill and sadly passed away. But more about Craig and Alex later.

Back at Durban City, Craig and I inherited a small, Irish coach who had been left behind when 'Budgie' Bryne left for Cape Town. His name was Harry Weir, and he'd spent most of his life in Rhodesia (now Zimbabwe).

I told Harry I wanted to build a team with local talent and asked if he knew of any. He told me he was aware of an exceptionally gifted young Durban-born goalkeeper playing for Highlanders FC, a predominantly black side based in Bulawayo. So we arranged to have a look at him.

The game had been underway for five minutes when the keeper came out to meet a cross. Instead of catching the ball, he headed it away. I looked aghast at Harry. 'You just wait and see...' he said.

Indeed, as the game progressed the goalie pulled off such a string of remarkable saves that on the strength of that single viewing, we took him to Durban. His name? Bruce Grobbelaar, who of course went on to become a world-class performer with Liverpool, winning the League championship six times, a hat-trick of FA Cups and the 1983/84 European Cup.

The contract I struck to secure Bruce's services at City had no frills attached, which was certainly quite different from the interesting deal he'd previously cut with Highlanders; as a signing-on clincher they had apparently offered him a cow, a sheep and a goat, and all the club needed to know was whether he wanted them delivered dead or alive. Bruce, apparently, decided to stick the billy goat in his back garden and the beef and mutton in his deep-freeze.

Due to his South African nationality – his family moved to Rhodesia when he was two – Bruce struggled to get a work permit in the UK for many years. He had far less of a problem getting into the States though, where I eventually took him, because apart from being a great keeper a little-known fact is that Bruce was also a top-flight baseball pitcher.

In South Africa at the time the Government was beginning to change its hardline stance and apartheid was gradually being dismantled. Sport in particular was early to react and football was soon becoming a predominantly black-powered organisation. Overnight the national league became multi-racial and twenty-one teams were thrown into one national league under black administration, with a couple of token Indian and White committee members.

At Durban City we had a man in charge of Bantu (Zulu) Welfare and Relationship and because we were short of a few quality front men, he convinced me the time was perfect to bring in a couple of Zulu players. No one had done this before but after much consideration I agreed.

My first move was to sign a black international from Amazulu called Moffat Zuma, who was keen to learn more about the European game as he liked our style of play. We paid R10,000 for him which was fine until we realised that 50,000 Amazulu supporters would be rather miffed at the deal.

Quite so, at his first training session around two hundred Amazulu fans turned up wielding machetes and knives threatening Moffat with all kinds of nasty retribution. Fortunately common sense prevailed and they left quietly but it was a situation I never wanted to witness again.

Later in the same season we took the team to play a cup tie in Johannesburg and stayed in a five-star hotel. We sat down for our pre-match meal and as apartheid was breaking down at the time, it was within the new laws that a black person could dine in a 'white' restaurant provided it had a five-star rating. But what we didn't realise was that if anyone in the restaurant objected, the black person could be asked to leave.

We were just finishing our meal when the head waiter told me that Mr Zuma must leave the restaurant as another diner had made a complaint. I was not at all happy and in no uncertain terms told him that Mr Zuma was a current international and part of a championship side and would therefore be finishing his meal and leaving the restaurant with his team-mates when he was good and ready. I'd barely finished making my point when the hotel manager arrived with four policemen, and the pair of us were dragged out of the restaurant, smacked around the head then dumped on the hotel steps. 'Nice to see things are changing,' I said. Moffat just smiled.

Moffat Zuma was an exceptionally intelligent man and became a very good friend. He did such a great deal to break down the barriers that had been put up in football. It was therefore an incredibly sad day for me when years later I heard that he had been murdered while protecting a youngster who was being attacked in the grocery store he owned.

Moffat was a massive loss.

The football was going really well in South Africa and by the mid-point of the season, the team was still unbeaten and striding away. A national side was selected which included eight of my players in the twenty-two man squad.

The wheelchair business had grown to the point where we were now employing two German toolmakers, six Indian machine operators and more than sixty Zulus covering a range of jobs. We moved into new premises which encompassed two huge factory floors and opened distribution outlets in Johannesburg, Cape Town, Port Elizabeth, Windhoek and Pretoria. My workload was becoming very difficult to manage but somehow we always seemed to meet the deadlines: it helped that I now had an assistant at both the football club and the wheelchair factory. The company then received another huge boost when we were awarded every contract to build wheelchairs in South Africa.

Many of the good times at Durban City revolved around the owner-come-chairman, who is without doubt the funniest character I have ever met in football. His main business was big event promotion, largely for boxing, hot rods and rock concerts. As a bachelor, ladies man and very smooth operator, I have enough stories about Norman Elliott to fill a book. But this is my book so I will just share a couple.

We were in a boardroom after a game – down in Cape Town I think – along with a reporter whom Norman had repeatedly crossed swords with over the previous twenty years. Everyone was standing around innocently nibbling vol-au-vents when out of the blue a right old barney kicked off between Norman and the hack, who met in a headlock and went spinning across the polished floor, taking out a couple of bystanders and the buffet for good measure. I've never seen anything like it in a boardroom since and I'm sure I never will.

Norman was a very heavy drinker and one afternoon I had arranged to meet him in our clubhouse. I was a couple of hours late as I'd been held up at work and when I arrived I found him asleep in his car with the doors locked and the windows closed. I banged and banged on the car but that didn't wake him so I decided to smash the side window. He remained dead to the world so I phoned for an ambulance, but the medics also failed to rouse him and refused to move his body until the fire brigade had sheared through the door of his silver Alfa Romeo.

Eventually cut out and taken to hospital, Norman, believe it or not, didn't wake up until the next morning. Talk about being paralytic. He wasn't very happy with the way I had reacted but as I pointed out afterwards, if he had signed the cheques and I could find the car keys, I would have left him there!

I liked Norman. He was a funny man and extremely good company. I also thought he was an intelligent man, until the day he called me to say that he was going to get married. He was in his mid-fifties then so I told him how pleased I was and that it was about time someone made an honest man of him. For a number of years he'd been going out with Danielle, a beautiful Jewish girl in her thirties, so I naturally assumed it was her he was marrying.

'I'm not marrying Danielle,' he said.

Pause.

'It's one of the barmaids.'

Now, we only had two barmaids at the club: Joyce, who was at least sixty five, and Marie Anne, her teenage niece.

'You've got to be joking,' I said. He wasn't and the wedding of Norman (pushing fifty-six) and Marie Anne (barely sixteen) was the most bizarre I've ever attended; I felt like a guest at Jerry Lee Lewis' reception. The marriage lasted all of eighteen months and luckily they didn't have a child. People do the strangest things at times.

There was a loud buzz around Durban City at the end of the season as we had won the Cup and remained unbeaten. One last result would see us make South African footballing history and our final game of the season, against African Wanderers, was played in front of Durban's biggest-ever gate.

Wanderers sat second from bottom in the league and

although we absolutely murdered them, we couldn't score and lost 1-0. Although I had won my first championship I was disappointed not to make the history books and to top the day off, when the players were carrying me around the stadium to celebrate our league title, they dropped me and I broke my wrist. Inevitably, we all got plastered that night: them in the pub, me in hospital.

8

Heartbreak

THEN our world was torn apart.

Claire had been complaining of feeling poorly and the family doctor advised she would need to have her tonsils removed. The date of the operation is an easy one to remember: it was the seventh of the seventh, nineteen seventy-seven.

However, five months later Claire's throat suddenly flared up again and she was rushed to hospital, where the doctors discovered two tumours and diagnosed them as lymphoma.

The cancer specialists in South Africa were not trained to deal with that particular strain of leukaemia at the time, so Claire was referred to Professor David Galton at the Hammersmith Hospital in London. It was the most heart-rending decision, but we realised that if our daughter was to receive the best attention, we would need to split the family. As such, Jill took Claire to England while Nick and I stayed in South Africa.

Professor Galton was a brilliant man and the world's leading authority and pioneer of leukaemia treatment. He carefully described a series of case studies in which children had suffered similar symptoms and slowly explained that we must face up to the fact that the maximum life span we could expect for Claire was two years. I cannot begin to put into words the crippling sense of hopelessness parents feel during such a nightmare: all you can do is hope and pray for a miracle.

We lost Claire on 11 January, 1979. She was twelve-and-a-half years old.

9

America Calling

WHEN Claire's condition was first diagnosed, Jill and I agonised over the best way to secure the finest care for our dear daughter. We concluded that our options were to return to England or take our chances in the United States, where several cancer specialists were offering alternative medicine. Around the same time one of my ex-players had recommended my coaching skills to a team in the American Soccer League. This was followed by a firm offer so, after carefully weighing everything up, we reached the conclusion that America would be a good move.

I remember Claire being particularly excited by the idea so I flew out to California to make sure that everything was satisfactory, signed the deal, then returned to South Africa to collect the family. So sadly though, Claire became too ill to travel and she was never to make the trip.

Nothing can prepare you for the loss of a child and the

sadness remains with you forever. Somehow life must go on though, and we knew we would never forget the wonderful years that our beautiful daughter was with us.

Claire had always wanted a horse but we never owned enough land to look after one. While I was in the States though, our best friends Val and Mark Lownds (the ex-Luton player) bought one for her and offered to stable it on their field. Claire christened him Charla – the Zulu word for 'free' – and I will always cherish the delight on her face when she told me on my return from America about the fun she'd been sharing with her four-hoofed friend.

With hindsight we should have found a way for Claire to own a horse earlier in her life and also put in a swimming pool, taken her to Disney World and done many, many other things. They are regrets I shall carry for the rest of my life.

Faced then with no choice but to move on, the three of us packed our suitcases and carrying the heaviest of hearts, we said our goodbyes in South Africa and left for America.

The Californian team I was in charge of was Sacramento Gold, who had just finished the season in bottom spot of the Eastern Section. My new job seemed rather like working for the League of Nations: the players were a mix of Brazilians, Mexicans, Argentinians and Uruguayans plus a couple of Americans, an Englishman and a Scot. Thankfully I had signed seven of my strongest players before leaving South Africa, but due to problems attaining their work permits they would not be arriving until at least two months into the season. I therefore had to start with what was already in place; something I was not looking forward to.

All I can really remember about my first six matches in charge is that we lost the lot. The stadiums were converted grid iron pitches, the crowds numbered less than a thousand and the standard of football was way below what I had been used to in South Africa – I felt my managerial career had taken at least ten steps backwards.

It had also dawned on me that Sacramento were not playing in the prestigious North American Soccer League, which I thought was the only league in the States, but the American Soccer League, which was relatively small fry. Mind you, one thing Americans are certainly good at is promotion, and each game Sacramento played drew huge TV and media coverage. And in America they love a juicy press conference, so I wasn't surprised when the knives were out at my first media call:

'Well coach, you've lost the first six, so will you be resigning? Or perhaps you can at least tell us what you're going to do?'

'The squad is just not good enough,' I answered. 'But as soon as my players arrive we will attack the league and if we don't win the championship I will cut off all the hair from my head, my chin (I wore a beard at the time) my chest and my legs. I'll even shave my wedding tackle.'

My promise of complete bodily depilation caused quite a stir: it made the national press and seriously upset the club's owners. Oops.

Sacramento is the capital of California and at that time the city had never produced a championship-winning team of any description; not in football, baseball, hockey, basketball or even tiddlywinks, which was amazing really.

My players duly arrived and at the same time I got really lucky when a scruffy but fit-looking lad pitched up and asked for a trial. His name was Guillermo Munguia and he told me he had been turning out for Real Madrid's reserves but was now travelling the world paying his way playing semi-professional football. He was and still is the only player in my thirty-five years of management that came via this route and could actually perform on the pitch, so suddenly I had eight new players. Guillermo – or Willy as we would grow to call him – was an out-and-out left winger.

Bursting with new blood the team went on an unbeaten run, won the play-offs and reached the championship final against the coyly-named Columbus Magic. Their manager was Keith Peacock and his assistant was Paul Taylor, both of whom of course later took charge at Gillingham. We won the game – which was played on Astro Turf – and became local heroes overnight. The turnaround in results ballooned our gate to more than four thousand and as the first championship-winning side in Sacramento's history we were invited to all kinds of flashy events.

The polish that gave Sacramento Gold its shine came from the club's owners; a pair of dark-suited Italians named John Andreotti and Sammy Cemo. There seemed to be nothing they couldn't arrange, which naturally led me to believe that they were part of the Mafia.

One day John called me into his office and declared that

he wanted to raise a million dollars to improve the team and thus secure back-to-back championships. To do so he proposed selling shares in the company and wanted yours truly to spearhead the drive.

After just two meetings we'd raised the money, but as the sale had been on the basis that if you bought 20,000 one-dollar shares or more you became an owner, we found ourselves with forty-six – yes, forty-six – different owners. Whatever, we began preparing for the season with $1.5 million in the bank, a crackerjack team and another $50,000 on its way from Tampa Bay for the sale of centre-forward Neil Roberts, who I had brought over from South Africa on a free.

America is very hot on its visitors carrying the correct work permit and with all the publicity the club was attracting, immigration officials decided to pay me a little visit. It should have been a stroll on the sidewalk but the club had not organised the correct paperwork so after much fuss and nonsense, I was shipped off to Canada for a fortnight while my visa was updated. Officially I had been deported so every time I returned to the States in later years, I always found myself carted off to that special room and given the third degree. Thankfully that doesn't happen anymore, although as you know I do still get the 'Is Your Name *Really* William Williams?' glare.

Although I carved a good side at Sacramento which played with great spirit, I did cross swords with one obnoxious little twerp called Willie Waddell. Now Willie was one of those players who you wouldn't call bad but he was just not quite as good as he thought he was. He was constantly knocking on my door telling me why he should play and what I didn't know about the game, until one day I had enough and sacked him.

A couple of weeks later Willie attacked me in a local bar and sadly I had to punch his lights out. That is never a nice thing to do and I was so sorry afterwards that I took him home, only to find myself on the end of a serious ear-battering from his wife.

Soon after, the general manager of Sacramento Gold called me into his office. Sitting alongside him was a plainclothes detective and a uniformed police officer. 'There's been a threat on your life and we're taking it seriously,' I was told.

Apparently someone – and I could only think of Willie, or perhaps his wife – had vowed to have me shot at one of the forthcoming games. The police and the club were quite concerned (well I suppose they had to be) but I wasn't too bothered as I knew that I hadn't upset anyone *that* much.

Preposterously though, the bullet-proof vests issued by the Californian cops were forged from old-fashioned chain mail and before each game I would climb into a leaden suit of armour, disguise it beneath my tracksuit, then sit in the stand man-marked by a couple of coppers. The searing heat would reach the eighties at times so I lost quite a few pounds in the process. The drama lasted a couple of months and made the national headlines but to this day I still have no idea whatsoever who wanted me gunned down.

Do I, Willie?

While preparing to defend our title with a handful of pre-season friendlies, a couple of players informed me that the payments on their club cars had not been honoured. This was followed by several squad members revealing that their rent had not been paid so I confronted Sacramento's owners, who palmed me off with some load of cock-and-bull. The alarm bells were ringing though and it was no surprise when, a month later, every salary, rental and expenses cheque bounced higher than Zebedee on Prozac.

I drove to the club offices (locked). I visited the owners' business premises (deserted). I called on the general manager (clueless). We went to the bank (open), where we discovered that the club's accounts had been plundered by John Andreotti (thieving bastard).

Consequently, Sacramento Gold went into administration and the Fraud Squad was called in. But it was a case of 'catch me if you can' and Andreotti had vanished faster than an unlocked Ferrari in Catford.

The club's other owner, Sammy Cemo, clearly had nothing to do with the theft and helped a number of the players get home, while Jill used the last of our savings to bail out a couple more who were left stranded. Unsurprisingly the press had a field day and playing with the club's name the headline splashed: *SACRAMENTO FOLD!*

Out of a job, it wasn't long before the family was struggling. Then I got a call out of the blue from Eddie Firmani, the former Charlton manager and Italian international, who wondered if I was interested in taking the team to play in Canada. I decided that I wasn't but around the same time I also heard from a very old friend, the ex-Gillingham winger

David Chadwick, who had landed the manager's job at Atlanta Chiefs and was looking for an assistant. That'll do us, I thought.

The Atlanta Chiefs were bottom of their league when I arrived in Georgia but the club had recently been taken over by CNN, the cable news network owned by media mogul Ted Turner. By nature, Mr Turner was demanding an immediate turnaround in results on the pitch.

David Chadwick and I got on terrifically well: he was a quiet, intelligent man and a tremendous coach, while I was the loud motivator who liked organising everything and showing the players how to win football matches. He was the boss and I respected that, but as this was my first job in football as an assistant it was tricky at times not having the final say.

The Chiefs had great owners, a great stadium, its own TV station and crowds of 8,000 plus: I felt back in the big time and everything looked bright again, the only hitch being that we quickly needed to attract some quality players.

As such David and I met with Ted Turner's right-hand man, Bob Wussler, who had just moved to CNN from CBS. Bob told us that he would happily stump up the cash to buy the best players available, as long as we made sure that they'd each played for their national side as international stars made the publicity machine run much smoother. This was David's first job as head coach (or 'manager' as we would call him) so he wasn't sure where to look for international players and was aware that even if he found them, they would cost the Earth (yes, even in those days).

David had a friend who used to manage Morecambe FC, Les Riggs, and Les knew everyone in football. David told him that we were looking for an English international and Les said that he had, just by chance, been speaking to one the very night before who was looking for a club. 'He's still got some legs on him but he'll be expensive,' Les warned us.

When we heard how much the player would cost we thought Les was joking but we got the green light from Ted Turner's office and two days later we had Brian Kidd on board. Meanwhile I zipped back to South Africa and signed four internationals, while David tracked down a couple in America. And we paid an absolute fortune for the signature of Branko Radovic, the Yugoslavian skipper who was playing for Red Star Belgrade. Suddenly the club was viable and fielding a good-looking side.

The thrust behind the Chief's commercial wing was supersonic: CNN was a massive operation that had just launched two of their own satellites and created the first twenty-four hour news service. Everything they did had to make business sense and football – or 'soccer' as they like to call it – was starting to take hold in certain States and sponsors were showing an interest. Soon our four main backers at the Chiefs were Coca-Cola, Budweiser, Delta Airlines and 7 Up. The team and management were backed by Adidas, who provided boots, kit, training equipment and luggage and even the coaches had sponsored suits and blazers, so one thing was for certain: when we went on the road we certainly looked smart.

Talking of Adidas, the brothers who founded the business, Adi and Rudolph Dassler – the latter of whom set up sportswear rival Puma following the siblings' bitter split – were both guests of Ted Turner at our opening game of the season, along with the heir to the Budweiser fortune. I can still remember David Chadwick and I agreeing that we wouldn't mind one per cent of their piggy banks.

The road trips the club embarked on were a new experience for me. We would fly to all our away games and were out of town for up to a week as we'd play two matches before coming home. It was certainly cost effective but an absolute nightmare trying to keep everyone interested and disciplined.

We made a good start to the season and had a good finish, ending as Eastern Conference champions and therefore qualifying for the regional quarter-finals. We drew the legendary New York Cosmos and although we lost I will always remember standing in the tunnel as the likes of Franz Beckenbauer, Johan Neeskens and the great man himself, Pele, came filing past me to warm up. I'd only ever seen such star players on the television and here I was about to begin a battle of wits with them. It was a wonderful dream come true and I loved every second.

Jill, Nick and I were enjoying life in Atlanta – we had settled into a house which backed onto a golf course in the wonderfully-named Snap Fingers Woods – so we decided it was time to plant some roots. Jill and I had already started the process in Sacramento but because the club had collapsed we were now in a new State and had to start all over again. Still, the management was happy to put the family through the Green Card process for permanent US residency.

In the meantime Bob Wussler was taking interest in my sales and project management skills and set about sending me on virtually every training course run by CNN. Bob was a very powerful man and believed that every person and every thing could be bought for a price. There again, he was instrumental in negotiating the marriage of Ted Turner to Jane Fonda – who believe it or not received $6 million to tie the knot – so perhaps he had a point.

There were two seasons in the North American League played with the same squad: the outdoor season lasted eight months and the indoor season three. With the outdoor league now finished, David and I prepared the players for a totally different experience – six-a-side continuous play indoors on an ice hockey rink that was covered with Astro Turf.

I had been doing a great deal of scouting for indoor players on my days off and had a clear strategy of how I thought we could win our league. I pitched my plan to David and we agreed to use a clock-timing system, which meant having the team work in pairs with each player on for two minutes, then off for two minutes. Simple.

The squad thought we were mad but I had noticed that any player who stayed on the pitch for more than two minutes would flag rapidly and his standard of play would plummet. Changeovers could be problematic at times – particularly if you were defending or were fifty metres from the bench – but as a general rule the idea worked well.

Indoor football was not very popular and we only had eight home games so the club's commercial department went into overdrive. I will never forget playing at the Omni Coliseum, home of Ted Turner's basketball team the Atlanta Hawks, which could hold 16,000 people. I'd taken Jill there to see the Jackson Five when we first arrived and could never imagine it being full for indoor football.

But we did just that on four occasions. The commercial team would stage a concert and we would play beforehand: normally we had between 8,000 and 11,000 to watch the match then as soon as it finished the pitch would be rolled away and those standing for the show would be let in to take the audience up to 16,000. The last game we played at the Omni was the national final in front of a full house. We beat Chicago Sting 6-3 and to this day I'm not sure if the crowd came to watch us or the Slim Whitman concert afterwards, which saw him backed by a forty-piece orchestra. It really was a great occasion and I was blown away by the power of event marketing.

It took just two seasons for David and I to take the Chiefs from the bottom of the table to the top and we'd also won two championships, although the National Conference title was seemingly owned by Cosmos.

The North American Soccer League was well run and a tremendous amount of cash was thrown at it. One aspect I particularly enjoyed was an event held once a quarter, when all the coaches would meet to swap ideas, hold training sessions and do a bit of horse-trading.

On one such weekend, Pele staged a shooting demonstration which, needless to say, was a joy to behold. The accuracy and power he displayed was breathtaking and I'd never seen anything like it before. And probably never will again.

To be honest, I was finding my role as David's assistant a right easy lark: restless nights sorting out players' problems were a thing of the past and all I had to do was keep everyone fit and confident and make sure the balance of the team was right. It was a good time: the Chiefs were winning, I was project managing at CNN and the family was loving life in Atlanta.

Then fell another bombshell.

10

Stones Throw

NOT content with sending a pair of satellites spinning into space, Ted Turner decided he wanted to launch a third. But they don't come cheap and he needed to find $72 million to pay for it.

Instead of instructing a secretary to rifle through his petty cash one afternoon, Ted unveiled widespread plans to raise the money by cutting costs within his sports franchises. That ultimately meant that everyone at Atlanta Chiefs was suddenly out of a job.

It could have been worse, I guess – I could have been back at Sacramento – but in much the same way as my time spent in California, after a couple of successful years under my belt I was being forced to start from scratch again. And, more importantly, where could the family move to this time?

I forgot to mention that seven months earlier Jill, who was thirty-nine at the time, had fallen pregnant. Once we'd picked ourselves off the floor – Nick was seventeen! – delight sank in and as far as we were concerned it was nothing short of a mini-miracle. Thanks to Ted's bombshell though the three and a half of us were left wondering what was waiting around the corner.

Two offers soon popped up: David Chadwick had landed a manager's job in Minnesota and asked me to join him, while Eddie Firmani was on the blower again trying to sell Canada.

Then I took a call from Billy Wheeler at the Kent Messenger Group. He was ringing on behalf of Jim Thompson, who wanted to know if I fancied returning to Maidstone United.

Years later Jim told me that he had always kept a close eye on my career abroad. To be honest Jill and I were ready to come home to be near her family for the birth of the baby. I also knew the club and the chairman and was ready to be totally in charge again.

Jim Thompson was a very ambitious man. He made it clear from the outset that he wanted The Stones to win the Alliance Premier League and eventually become a professional Football League club. He was aware of my background in project management and marketing so I was offered a full-time position that gave me full responsibility for not only the team but also the club's commercial operation.

When I arrived at London Road in November 1981 the side was facing relegation. There were plenty of games in which to pick up points but what I inherited was probably the worst team I had the misfortune of being involved with since I arrived in Sacramento.

The first match I took charge of was away at Altrincham. On the way up to Manchester our goalkeeper at the time, Dickie Guy – the Wimbledon legend who famously saved Peter Lorimer's penalty at Elland Road when the Dons held Leeds to an FA Cup draw in 1975 – told me that we were about to face the nastiest team in the league and the nastiest player-manager around; a man named John King. 'Just keep him away from me, boss,' Dickie said. 'He frightens me to death.'

I spoke to King in the tunnel before the game. He didn't know me or how I set out my teams of course but that didn't stop him spouting off about how all Southerners were as soft as you-know-what and that my lot were no different.

While managing in the States I had been using a continental three-at-the-back system with either five across the middle and two forward, or four in midfield with three up front. Hoping to catch out King I wound up the team like clockwork rabbits and played 3-4-3. We gave a great display and during the 2-1 victory showed some grit and put in a few tackles. I was delighted with the boys and made a point of seeing John King afterwards to explain that it was not always about being soft or hard but how good your players are and the system they are taught to play in. He acknowledged his earlier lack of professionalism and we remained good friends for the following twenty years.

In February the surprise new addition to the Williams' family arrived, James Richard, and the family moved into a house in Ditton. Finally it seemed that a bit of stability had entered the household.

The rest of the season at London Road was hard going but we achieved what we set out to do and The Stones avoided the drop. It was therefore time to start re-building the side in preparation for the next campaign – I can't remember how many of the squad I kept but I know it wasn't many.

Jim Thompson was not the interfering chairman many thought he was. Yet he was demanding and expected results. His two main goals in football were no secret: to get Maidstone into the Football League and head up the Football Association and change the image of football.

When I joined The Stones as manager there were two coaches already in place, John Ryan and Duncan McLaughlin, and although they were good men they were not what I was looking for. What I yearned for was a player-coach who could transfer what I said onto the field.

I looked everywhere and eventually spoke to Gordon Taylor, who was now working for the Professional Footballers' Association. I'd got to know Gordon in my time at West Brom when he was playing for Birmingham City, and he told me that Peter Taylor had been freed by Leyton Orient. I thought the ex-Spurs and England winger was a little out of our league – literally – but I gave him a call anyway.

The first thing Peter said was that he was looking for a position outside of football as he had just had two hernia operations and wasn't sure about his playing future. Nevertheless I offered him a two-year contract and a signing on fee, also giving him the freedom to look for a part-time job.

Two weeks later Peter signed. I had taken such a gamble –

I wouldn't do it again on an injured player – but he recovered fully and was an absolute sensation for us. He was far too good for our level but you never heard me complaining.

Peter and I got on well and we have remained friends throughout his wonderful career. Although he only took charge of the full England side for one match as caretaker manager – the 1-0 defeat away to Italy in November 2000 – Peter showed his visionary skills by handing David Beckham the captain's armband for the first time and selecting six players who were still eligible for the Under 21s, namely Gareth Barry, Jamie Carragher, Kieron Dyer, Rio Ferdinand, Emile Heskey and Seth Johnson. Mind you, although I could tell that Peter had the makings and talent to become a great coach while he was at Maidstone, the seemingly laid-back Essex lad was somewhat temperamental when he first started at London Road...

One evening the two of us were coaching the team, which we had split into four groups. Each group would eventually rotate to Peter who was working on some rather complicated throw-ins in the final third. At one point I looked across the pitch and saw Peter's group standing around without him. 'He's gone inside to change,' they told me, so I went back to what I was doing. I looked over again a little later and Peter was still nowhere to be seen. 'He got changed and went home,' the players said.

There was a big inquest at the next training session: Peter had got the needle because the players couldn't execute what he wanted them to do and had called them a few unpleasant names before showering and naffing off home. It only happened once though and he soon apologised, having learnt that there are different levels in football and you have to accept players' weaknesses as much as their strengths.

With Peter's help the team improved week-on-week and was becoming a force to be reckoned with. The structure was good and with an improving scouting system we were attracting quality players: we managed to lure fireman-come-goal-machine John Bartley from Welling, agile loose cannon Stephen John 'Billy' Hughes from Wimbledon plus England non-league internationals John Watson, Derek Richardson and Brian Thompson, who played his testimonial at London Road in 1985 against Spurs.

We later landed prolific striker Steve Butler who I think holds some kind of record for bagging eight goals for Cambridge over the Easter weekend of 1994. Steve of course later returned to score goals for Maidstone in the Kent League and was an innocent bystander during the disastrous management reign of Andy Ford in the long hard winter of 2010, which saw The Stones relegated for the first time.

Although my rebuilding of the squad was based on offering good salaries to attract quality players, I found there was cashback available if you looked on your own doorstep...

Our reserves were rather ordinary at the time but watching them one afternoon it was hard not to notice our wafer-thin right-winger flying up and down the line and crossing balls onto the penalty spot. I stuck him straight into the first team and he proved nothing short of marvellous, winning us game after game as we rose further up the league. David Holmes, incidentally, later became a Kent bobby.

With class on the pitch and gates increasing off it – we were now averaging around a thousand – everyone was happy. But the pressure suddenly started to hit home: I hadn't imagined being in a position to challenge for the title in my first full season, particularly as the club had finished fourth from bottom the previous year under Barry Watling.

Come the final game of the season, to win the Alliance Premier we needed to beat Scarborough five-nil at home and hope that Enfield slipped up at Runcorn. We had a huge crowd for the game and at the final whistle had kept a clean sheet while hitting Scarborough for six.

As we paraded off the field it was announced over the public address system that Enfield had lost 2-1 at Runcorn. We were champions! The crowd exploded and there was mayhem as they invaded the pitch.

However, by the time we'd reached the dressing rooms, a very apologetic Jim Thompson broke the news that Enfield had actually equalised in the ninety-sixth minute and that we had been pipped to the 1982/1983 league title by a point. It was a huge disappointment but we'd had an amazing season.

Yet the excitement was far from over – Enfield's ground was deemed too poor to meet the standard required for promotion and we therefore won the right to apply for election to the Football League, potentially replacing one of the bottom four sides in the Fourth Division.

In those days you had to be voted into the League by the

member clubs, so Jim launched a top-drawer campaign and we contacted every club individually to seek support. The day of the decision finally arrived and the vote went as follows:

CLUB	FINAL POSITION	VOTES
Blackpool	21st (Fourth Division)	52
Crewe Alexandra	23rd (Fourth Division)	49
Hereford United	24th (Fourth Division)	49
Hartlepool United	22nd (Fourth Division)	36
Maidstone United	2nd (Alliance Premier)	26

Clearly we had lost by some margin and were therefore denied membership of the Football League. On the plus side, the members and committee stated quite publicly that if we went away and returned as champions the following season, we would be looked upon far more favourably. So the die was cast and we knew what we had to do.

Thanks to the maddeningly haphazard system of seeking election to the Football League that The Stones had just fallen foul of, Jim spent much of his time trying to promote the construction of a pyramid of non-league teams that could encompass automatic promotion from the bottom tier to the top. We often spoke about the clubs that had consistently snubbed the idea and I recall that Bishop Auckland FC was the last to sign up – and that was under protest.

I remember Jim phoning me late one evening to tell me

he was driving to Gateshead to try to persuade the Auckland chairman to agree to the idea of a football pyramid. Jim asked if I would go with him as co-pilot as he'd have to turn straight around and drive back.

'What time are you leaving?' I asked.

'Three o'clock tomorrow morning; the meeting's at nine.'

We talked tactics and strategy all the way there but by lunchtime there was still no agreement. Jim and I drove home not saying a word to each other for the entire journey.

While planning his reorganisation of non-league football Jim had been searching for a new name for the Alliance Premier League and I told him about the various Conferences in the States. He liked the sound of it so I suppose I had a small hand in the Alliance Premier being renamed the Conference in 1986. The system works very well today, to the point where automatic promotion to the Football League has been achieved.

We assembled a strong side for the start of the 1983/1984 campaign and The Stones looked like the team to beat. Throughout the season we put in some excellent performances and were well on track to take the title.

The club also began a knack of reaching the Third Round of the FA Cup. We enjoyed many great FA Cup ties in my time – the away games at Watford in 1987 and Sheffield United the following year were truly wonderful days out for the fans – but this year's campaign was to prove my most disappointing.

Our First Round tie was against Exeter City at their place.

We got a draw then beat them 2-1 at home in the replay thanks to goals by Paul Lazurus and Mickey Dingwall. We then edged past Worcester City 3-2 at London Road and sat in the dressing room eagerly awaiting the Third Round ties.

In those days the draw was made on the radio at five o'clock, and you could have cut the tension in the dressing room with a shin guard as we all prayed for Manchester United or Arsenal. Then our name finally came out of the hat: away to Fourth Division Darlington. I had sat with many teams over the years as the Third Round ties were announced, but never before had I experienced complete silence when you discover who you've got. We were, of course, stuffed 4-1.

Jim Thompson was a fan of the FA Cup but the most important silverware to him was the Kent Senior Cup. He loved the look of the trophy and the only time we ever fell out was over that competition. Jim always wanted the full first team out on the park and I liked to use the competition to give the fringe players a game.

One freezing evening in January he insisted that our strongest side should play against Ramsgate who I had been told were turning out a scratch team. The ground was rock hard but their youngsters flew across the icy surface while my prima donnas took a stroll in the park. We lost 4-1.

Jim didn't question my selection again for a long time, until he demanded to know why his favourite player – the ex-Millwall and Gillingham midfielder Dean White – wasn't getting more playing time. We must have lost a couple of games otherwise the conversation would never have taken place. Whatever, I thought it was high time Jim got a feel of what life on the bench was all about, so I suggested he took charge of a league match down at Bath while I went scouting elsewhere. Bath must have been an easy game or I would never have sent him down. Regardless, he hated every single minute and never questioned my decisions again.

I wouldn't say that we were running away with the 1983/1984 title – in fact we were fifteen points adrift of Nuneaton at Christmas – but following many more great displays we became national non-league champions for the first time after whacking six past Telford in front of more than 2,500 jubilant fans at London Road. John Bartley hit a hat-trick, there were a couple of strikes from Andy Rollings and a vintage effort by Peter Taylor. The players were naturally nervous before the match, but I rated their performance as almost perfect.

Around this time two of the club's great supporters, Pat Gallagher of the Gallagher Group and John Baxter of Britelite Windows, became directors and are still heavily involved in the club all these years later. However, when you win promotion I have always believed that it is without doubt the players' day as it is them who win the championship. Supporters, managers and coaches come close behind though and it's impossible to explain the unbridled joy a manager feels when you win a league. And I have always loved that feeling.

Despite winning the title, it was no time to rest on our laurels, so the very next day I urged everyone to concentrate on the job in hand – preparing another powerful campaign to seek promotion to the Football League. We had achieved what the committee had asked us to do and were now back expecting to be elected as champions.

But there were rumblings afoot. Jim went away on business and while his back was turned the rest of the board members issued themselves with new shares and effected a coup, with Cyril Nicholls taking over as chairman. Cyril was a recently-appointed director and had dug the club out of a financial hole by loaning £50,000. He clearly wasn't short of a bob or two as he owned a number of successful companies. I took him to be a genuine person.

I shall never forget the day Cyril took over. I was called into his office and told that in future I was only to make contact with him direct, not through Jim Thompson. Cyril then went on to say that he immediately wanted me to drop one particular member of the first team as he had heard on the grapevine that the lad was playing away from his wife. I suggested that if that was the only reason for dropping him then he should consider dropping at least another half-a-dozen.

Cyril didn't think it was very funny and he certainly didn't smile when I said that if he wanted such involvement with the team, he would have to pay me up and I would make a statement to the press that Cyril Nicholls was selecting the side from now on. Cyril soon reconsidered his demand though, which probably had something to do with the fact that we were sitting pretty on top of the league at the time.

Regardless of the power struggles at the club, the day came for us to return to meet the Football Association at Lancaster Gate. This time we all felt confident that promotion was imminent.

As before, the club had been pitched a first-class campaign to the league clubs and feedback suggested around seventy-five per cent of them would this time vote in favour of accepting us into the Fourth Division.

This was the final count:

CLUB	FINAL POSITION	VOTES
Chester City	24th (Fourth Division)	52
Halifax Town	21st (Fourth Division)	52
Rochdale	22nd (Fourth Division)	50
Hartlepool United	23rd (Fourth Division)	32
Maidstone United	1st (Alliance Premier)	22

As a result, all four Football League teams were re-elected and Maidstone United was, for the second time in two years, denied membership of the Football League. That led Jim and I to reach one simple conclusion about the honesty and parentage of the committee members: *What a bunch of lying bastards!*

Jim said a few words expressing his disappointment at the vote then I stood up and blasted the members with both barrels, for which I was asked to leave the meeting. I told them I was going anyway. I could never understand how Jim could remain so calm under this type of treachery.

Not long after this tremendous disappointment my old friend Mark Lownds phoned from South Africa to ask me to consider going into business with him. As Durban City were also looking for a part-time manager and my current contract at Maidstone was up, I decided – after hours of painstaking deliberation – that it was once again time for a fresh start. I regarded Maidstone United as a great and wonderful club, but I had done just about all I could to get them promoted and as for those bureaucratic berks in charge of the Football League, I didn't want to waste one more minute of my time on them.

So I told the board I was finished. They were not happy and made me a magnificent offer to stay, but my mind was made up and after much heartache, we parted company.

11

I Didn't Predict a Riot

EVEN though I recommended Kettering Town's Peter Morris as the best man to replace me at London Road, the board decided it wanted to lure Barry Fry from Barnet.

Whatever, it was none of my business anymore so I left them to it and we sold our house in Ditton, said goodbye to our folks (again!) and once more left for South Africa.

The changes which had taken place in the six years we'd been away were amazing. The biggest difference I noticed was in football: the National League was now totally multi-racial although the majority of teams were all black. Meanwhile the administration had changed from multi-racial to all black, which wasn't a bad thing but certain customs and standards were very different and took a bit of getting used to.

When I signed to become manager of Durban City for the second time, I soon realised they were certainly not the force they once were. I was also invited to lend a hand coaching the

Amazulu team and I'll never forget flying to my first away fixture with them.

Or not, as the case was, because when we arrived at the airport the players decided that the coach and I were 'bad medicine' and believed it would be disastrous if we travelled on the same plane as them. So off they went and we followed on the next flight. Not being brought up with witchcraft made it very hard to understand but the hoodoo voodoo never really bothered me, as I was always very superstitious and would go through the same ritual before a game (I always wore the same shirt on an unbeaten run washed, of course, between matches by my wonderful wife).

The family moved into a lovely home near the beach and we had the place totally refurbished. Jill went to the local RSPCA and rescued the most beautiful Great Dane; Nick had joined the army and James was into everything as three-year-olds are. Life was good for us even though South Africa seemed even hotter this time around due to the humidity from living near the sea.

The wheelchair operation had sold out to a Japanese company in my absence (I never saw or heard of the Deane family again) so the business side of my life involved the production and selling of light fittings. For the first time though I wasn't enjoying trying to sell something: I think the problem was that I didn't know enough about the different products and found myself tied in knots during conversations about the technology. Regardless, two events then occurred that made a huge impact on the rest of my life...

Durban City were playing at home against African Wanderers. Most of our supporters were still of Indian origin and the Government had decided to scrap segregation inside the country's stadia for the first time. We hadn't even reached half-time when a riot erupted in the South Stand, and I was horrified to witness Wanderers' supporters throwing a great number of our fans from the upper tier onto the concrete slabs some thirty feet below. Half-a-dozen people were killed and it took several hours to stop the violence.

Then, some months later, the final nail was put in my football career in South Africa.

We arrived to play a friendly in one of the townships at about half past twelve, where we found a pre-match curtain-raiser being played in front of around 4,000 people. Come half past two there were 20,000 fans in the stadium, all of whom were in good humour waiting for the teams to come out. But just as the players and I were leaving the dressing room, a policeman explained that a massive demonstration was on its way to the ground, and the horde was expecting to persuade the spectators to abandon the game and join them at the funeral of a local Government official.

Within minutes there were 40,000 people outside the stadium trying to enlist the 20,000 inside. Huge rocks began raining down and hundreds of rioters tooled up with knives, machetes and sticks steamed into the stadium. Bedlam broke out and we were escorted back to the dressing room and told not to worry as the army was on its way.

It is the only time I have genuinely thought my life was

in danger: the ruckus was unbelievable and I honestly thought we hadn't got long. Then a couple of officials from the opposition arrived and told us to follow them and if possible could we please be quick about it, as if they needed to flaming well ask that!

At the end of the tunnel two soldiers armed with machine guns quickly loaded all our players and management into two anti-tank transporters. I can't tell you what was happening outside: I could only imagine the huge vehicles smashing anything that got in their path as they ploughed through the mass of people. Every few minutes blasts of ammunition would fill the air which we were later told was the police shooting over the heads of the rioters, who were running for cover knowing full well that the next blast would be aimed at them.

Although these were the only two violent incidents I witnessed on my return to South Africa, the biggest problem for me was that I wasn't at all convinced that the game's officials weren't in somebody's back pocket. Moreover the standard of play was much worse than I was used to and I reminded myself that I had been searching for something secure and stable – which was certainly not going to be football in South Africa.

While overseas I always had the local British papers shipped out to me so I was well aware that Maidstone United under Barry Fry were struggling and had been in the bottom three for a long time: I believe the boys in the Shed at the Athletic Ground were subsequently prone to chant: 'He's fat, he's round, he tried to take us down, Barry Fry, Barry Fry.'

I also had a cherished reminder with me in Durban of my time in Kent as I had been presented with a wonderful cup for being named Manager of the Year of the Alliance Premier League in 1984. The trophy was mine to keep for a year but as I had moved to South Africa I thought I could get away with having it on my shelf forever: after all, the Alliance was being re-named the Conference so surely they would need a new cup anyway?

But of course I was dealing with Jim Thompson, the best football administrator I ever met. One day I answered my front door in Durban to be faced with two officials calling on behalf of the league chairman. They cut to the chase: 'Jim wants the Manager of the Year trophy back.'

I told them they must be joking and that I had sent it to England via airmail several months earlier.

'We want to come in and have a look around,' they insisted.

'Don't you believe me?' I said.

'No.'

The conversation soon contained threats similar to those employed by bailiffs but to this day that pair of officials never knew that the huge Great Dane I threatened them with would more likely have licked them to death than taken a chunk out of their shins.

It was not the last I was to see of those officials though: they came back several months later to see if I was interested in returning to manage Maidstone United, as the club was on the verge of relegation and Jim had decided that even if Barry Fry managed to keep the team up they were parting company as the appointment had not worked out. The offer was a good one but it was made with three games left and the club needing four points and a few goals to avoid the drop.

Not for the first time Jill and I talked about moving, which was made easier as our immigration had not yet been completed. We were both also missing things about the UK, our remaining families in particular. Durban City were in a respectable mid-table position and Mark Lownd's business was doing well – he was very cross when I told him I was leaving but we remain good friends to this day – so it didn't really take very long to reach the decision.

I therefore phoned Jim and told him I would return to Kent but on three conditions: firstly the club must stay in the Alliance Premier (which was known as the Gola League in 1985/1986 for sponsorship reasons), secondly I wanted total control of the team and thirdly, I would be allowed to keep the Manager of the Year trophy. He agreed.

While Jim was on the phone he told me the club had just signed Mark Cooper on loan from Spurs and that he was 'the business'. I doubt most Gillingham fans would agree: Mark went to Priestfield soon after for a then club record fee of £102,500 but he struggled and soon became labelled a high-priced flop.

It looked very much as though The Stones were doomed for the drop until their away fixture at Enfield at the end of April. I can clearly remember the match as I had telephoned John Still – who'd been a friend for years – and asked him to go to the game and give me an update every fifteen minutes.

John reported via a crackly phone line that Mickey Joyce nicked us a pair of goals in the second half to give Maidstone an amazing 3-1 win against the team who had already won the title. And when John confirmed the Stones' survival after the final match of the season, in which Clive Green hit a hat-trick at London Road against Dartford in a 5-1 victory, it was a massive relief after much unnecessary stress on the end of a telephone some nine hundred miles away.

Whatever, with my conditions met, I was on my way back to dear old Maidstone United.

12

Rolling Stones

AS THE Stones had needed goal difference to scrape their way to safety at the end of the 1985/1986 season, there was a mammoth job to be done when I took the helm for the following campaign. A big boost was that in my absence from Britain, Jim had convinced the powers-that-be to finally open the door to automatic promotion and relegation between the Conference and the Football League, which was obviously a major incentive after enduring the ludicrous bureaucracy that effectively made me quit English football two years earlier.

There had also been big changes at London Road, the most significant being that Jim had regained control of the club and the directors involved in the coup had fallen on their swords.

Inspired by Jim's ambition, the new board were similarly desperate for Football League status but the Athletic Ground was, for a whole host of reasons – dilapidated infrastructure and a dearth of parking top of the list – inadequate for the

Football League. The club was therefore forced to consider all available options to re-house within the borough.

I still have – probably like many fans of a certain age – the brochure identifying the stack of potential sites that we professionally investigated, which numbered a grand total of forty-nine. Yet, for one reason or another – and for reasons that nobody could or ever will comprehend – not one single site was considered suitable by the council. At the same time several companies were knocking at the club's door keen to purchase our land at London Road.

The 1986/1987 Conference season was also a topsy-turvy affair on the field but we somehow managed to finish in third position and at least create an air of respectability on the pitch. No thanks to our away fixture at Northwich Victoria in early November, mind, which brought ridicule upon the team and the club.

We arrived at their ground around one o'clock to learn that four of their side had been injured in a traffic accident and they were therefore asking for the match to be postponed. That was fine with us, but the League insisted that as long as Northwich had seven players fit and available, the game must go ahead.

We sat in the dressing room for three hours and the match eventually kicked off at half-four. During the delay our hosts had been granted special permission to sign four local lads on the hoof, one of whom had been literally sinking beer and playing pool in the bar.

But by the time we crossed the white line our boys were not

up for the game and didn't want to play: we were terrible and the lad from the bar ran us ragged. We drew one-all and the national press grabbed the story.

Blimey, the news even reached America:

'Three sports enthusiasts lived out every fan's fantasy on Saturday when, in an unlikely turn of events, they left the stands to play for a short-handed soccer team.

Illness left Northwich Victoria with only eight players, and chairman Derek Nuttall appealed over the public address system to the 738-strong crowd: "Does anyone want a game?"

Sunday league amateurs Steve Garnett, Rick Parkin and Mike Fogg were put in the line-up and helped Northwich hold heavily-favoured Maidstone United to a 1-1 tie.'

LOS ANGELES TIMES, NOVEMBER 10, 1986

I took the embarrassing result very personally and for the only time in my career I called the team in for training on the Sunday morning.

Then, some weeks later, I was in the boardroom after a game and when I nipped to the loo I overheard one director say to another: 'I think Bill's lost it; he's not what he used to be. Perhaps we should think about replacing him.' Their attitude soon changed when I confronted them, and of course they denied ever saying it.

Although things were looking rather rocky off the field, we

had reached the Third Round of the FA Cup and in January faced a spine-tingling trip to play First Division Watford.

And what a day that was. A colder afternoon you could not imagine and the pitch was harder than Mark Lazarus. But the welcome from our hosts was magnificently warm and before the game Watford presented us with a silver salver to mark the occasion (we gave them a 'bronze' shield).

Around 4,000 Maidstone fans travelled to Vicarage Road, many of whom filled two specially chartered trains. In the crowd of nearly 16,000 there were just two arrests and even British Rail (remember them?) gave Maidstone United fans a 'verbal bouquet' for behaving like very good boys and girls on their big awayday.

We took our own ball boys to the game and before the teams came out, they deftly executed Jim Thompson's plan of wishing his opposing chairman – millionaire rock musician Elton John – a speedy recovery from his recent throat operation by holding up a placard saying: Elton: Get Well Soon! You'd be amazed how long it took to rehearse.

Our ball boys then clapped the team out onto the pitch. Mind you, after our valiant 3-1 defeat, it was the Watford players who clapped our boys off it.

Reporter Tony Banks summed up the occasion well:

'Despite the fact that they lost, the day out at Watford can be counted as probably the most memorable in Maidstone United's 90-year history.

It was the first time they had met a First Division club

in a competitive match, and the moment when Steve Galloway's hooked volley zipped past Tony Coton and into the Watford net to give Stones the lead will remain in many minds for a long time.'

KENT MESSENGER, JANUARY 16, 1987

And for the record, here's what yours truly had to say for himself at the post-match press conference:

'For the first 43 minutes we were feeling very pleased with ourselves. I thought we contained them well and created three real scoring chances from which we scored one.

'We would like to strangle our 'keeper [Derek Richardson] *who should have held on to the ball which allowed Falco to score.*

'You have got to give credit to Graham Taylor for his substitution at half-time. It threw us completely. He put our newest player [Jesse Roast] *against John Barnes.*

'Their first goal was a body blow. Until then we had done very well. Despite the score, it was a tremendous day for us. The players were singing away in the dressing room afterwards, even though they had lost.'

In his own post-match interview, England manager-to-be Graham Taylor praised our courageous performance:

'Full credit must go to Maidstone for the way they played. I have seen many lower division sides who are not as good as them,' he told reporters.

He then came out with a pearl that was worth an entry in *Private Eye's* Colemanballs: 'When Maidstone scored, I knew we had to get two.'

Great maths, Graham!

Despite finishing third in the league and enjoying a memorable cup run, which raked in more than £40,000, Jim spoke to me at the end of the season and gave me the impression he wanted me to concentrate solely on the club's commercial activities. He asked if I was ready to step away from the team, move upstairs and become an Associate Director (bearing in mind that I was already General Manager, Secretary, Team Manager and Commercial Manager). I asked for a couple of days grace before discussing it further.

After a long hard think the only local man who I felt could take The Stones into the Football League was John Still, who was then managing Leytonstone and Ilford. Jim agreed and John was keen so for the 1987/1988 campaign, we quickly rejigged the management structure with me in charge of the day-to-day running and commercial affairs and John as team manager. Meanwhile, the directors would concentrate on building a new stadium (ha-ha-ha).

John Still and I got on well from the moment we started working together. Our first move was to buy Ken Charlery, Gary Cooper and Dave Mehmet from Fisher Athletic for £35,000, the most the club had ever shelled out in the transfer market (the previous highest being £8,000 for Clive Green from Yeovil Town in 1982).

Talking of transfers the system today is so much easier than it was in the past, thanks largely to the use of emails and faxes. In the days before such technology, I remember a right old palaver when we signed Gerry Pearson from Weymouth.

I had agreed a price of £4,500 with them on the Thursday but wanted Gerry to play on the Saturday. So off I went to Weymouth late in the afternoon with Jim Dawkins (one of the directors) and we eventually got Gerry's signature at elevenish in the evening. We immediately turned around and began the four-hour drive back home. I had a quick bite to eat then drove straight up to Lancaster Gate to post the forms through the FA's door. I got back at half-six and we received confirmation that Gerry could play at midday on the day of the match. Today it's just a couple of emails and the job is done in half-an-hour – no fun at all.

Leading the line of prospective purchasers for the Athletic Ground was furniture giant MFI and an emergency board meeting was convened when they pitched their offer of £2.5 million. Our options were to therefore stay where we were and take our chances, or accept the money and ground share if we were unable to secure a suitable site to build a new stadium. Although no one had considered what would happen if we gained promotion to the Football League, the resolution was unanimous and we set about the task of seeking a ground share agreement.

Now, dear reader, hold on to your bobble hat because what I am about to spill has been a closely guarded secret for many years. Nevertheless I think every Stones' fan deserves to know what very nearly took place back then...

Desperate for a local landlord, we approached Gillingham. They said that they were more than happy for Maidstone to move in with them at Priestfield, but that we would, quite naturally, have to wait until Hell had frozen over.

However, the following day a group of their supporters approached us to say that they thought the ground share was a sensible idea and would therefore be prepared to offer us their individual stakes in the club. This prompted another meeting: at the time we had a number of Gillingham shareholders on our board and they felt that by combining their own shares and those on offer from the supporters, we could not only win a vote but also take control of the club.

Believe it or not then, some weeks later Maidstone United potentially owned enough of a stake in Gillingham to become the majority shareholder. There were a few legal issues that would need to be ironed out, but on paper the ownership was feasible. Amazingly, with less than twenty-four hours to go before Gillingham's Annual General Meeting, we were poised to spark the biggest controversy in the history of Kent football.

Until, that is, I received a call from Jim Thompson. He told me he had decided not to go ahead with the takeover as he felt it would not work and there would be too much bad feeling. He added that although we didn't have many friends at Gillingham, he didn't want to lose the ones we had.

I have to say that it was without doubt the correct

decision. Can you imagine The Stones owning The Gills with just a token member or two on the board? Even more of a potential nightmare was that Priestfield would have effectively been split in half, with Maidstone owning the Main Stand and the Town End and Gillingham owning the Rainham End and the Stanley Stand. Only a very brave man could manage that.

As a side note, Maidstone's potential ownership of Gillingham would certainly have silenced their fans: following the sale of the Athletic Ground they dubbed their local rivals 'The Squatters', but if the takeover of Gillingham by Maidstone had gone ahead as planned, they would have been the ones who were squatting!

With the sale of the Athletic Ground to MFI soon signed and sealed – the final game was on Saturday 23 April 1988: a 4-2 victory over Stafford Rangers that saw us finish the season ninth in the Conference – we had still been unable to secure a new site in the town.

Thankfully though, Dartford Football Club agreed to let us share their ground at Watling Street. But not unlike London Road, Watling Street was not up to scratch so we had to spend and spend again to raise it to the rigorous standards set by the Football League. Naturally that put a sizeable dent in the money we'd received from the sale and I think the final bill came to around £850,000. What I am sure of is that our financial boys who did the sums each year reckoned we would have a maximum of five years on the budgeted losses before we ran out of money.

On the pitch the 1988/1989 campaign began superbly and the signing of Mark Gall from Greenwich Borough had proved to be a brilliant call: the combination of Smokey and Steve Butler was frightening defences to death. Throughout the season the team ploughed on winning football matches and my relationship with John was as strong as ever.

We did fall out once over team selection though. During the season's run-in we were playing a vital game away at Kidderminster Harriers. One of our key players, Dave Mehmet, was hobbling on a hamstring injury but John was still planning to play him. I suggested that he couldn't start an injured player.

'Yes I can and I will,' he said, adding that Mehmet was a better player on one leg than most of the others were on two. I daren't put into print what I said to John but in fairness he stuck to his guns and Dave lined up at the kick-off.

We won a corner early on which Mehmet took. He dropped it right on Steve Butler's bonce. One-nil. Ten minutes later Mehmet played a great ball over the top into Mark Gall's stride. Two-nil. Then, just before half-time, Mehmet stroked a free-kick into the top corner to put us three-up. As the players walked off for a well-earned cup of tea, John looked up at me in the stand. 'Shall I take him off now?' he said.

We won the game 6-3 with Mehmet our star turn and needless to say, the slice of humble pie I was served after the match was rather on the thick side.

We reached the final of the Kent Senior Cup that year (Jim was delighted of course) and shortly before Steve Butler's extra-time winner at Priestfield against Welling United, the news that we were all awaiting filtered through – Kettering had lost to Enfield, making us Conference champions once again. At long last Maidstone United had won automatic promotion to the Football League.

It took at least ten minutes for the news to sink in but then the celebrations were incredible and I shall never forget the unbridled joy of knowing what we had achieved and what we had to look forward to. Thousands lined the streets of Maidstone a week later to cheer the open-top bus that was carrying the team, officials and both pieces of silverware we had won on the same day. But no sooner had the jubilation subsided it was back to serious business: football can be a brutal game at times.

Talking of which, soon afterwards another board meeting was called, to which I was not invited. To this day I do not know if any skulduggery took place but John Still was offered a one-year contract which he apparently turned down. Accordingly the manager's job was offered to ex-Gillingham boss Keith Peacock, who jumped at the chance to lead The Stones into the Fourth Division.

John spoke to me afterwards and said that the offer had not been good enough for him to leave his current job as an executive manager. My personal opinion is that he was shafted, as the board didn't think he was an experienced enough manager. I guess we shall never know the truth.

Whatever, with a new management team in place and a public promise from the Mayor of Maidstone to help the club find a way back to the town, we were looking forward to the most exciting season in the Stones history. It felt like a real adventure into the unknown.

I was now general manager and secretary and Jim was dealing directly with manager Keith Peacock so it seemed my involvement with the team was over. That obviously meant there was no longer any pressure on me to win football matches, which was a very strange feeling indeed.

Our first game in the Fourth Division of the 1989/1990 campaign was away to Peterborough, and the excitement of that day has always stayed with me. In fact the pleasure lasted for the whole season as every match was a completely new experience. Sitting in the stand not needing to make sure the team performed each week didn't seem quite right, but it was certainly beneficial for my blood pressure.

There was also excitement on the home front that season. Four years earlier, while serving in the 2nd Tank Regiment, Nick had returned home from Canada to pop the question to his lovely girlfriend Samantha, who he'd been stepping out with since his teens. Now they were tying the knot and on 28 July 1990, they married at our local church and our eldest flew the family nest.

Back at the football, we had a great first term in the Fourth Division and following a shaky start came close to achieving back-to-back promotions by reaching the play-offs. We lost to eventual winners Cambridge United in a most dramatic two-legged semi-final in which Cambridge striker Dion Dublin came good twice in the second period of extra time.

Our (short) time in the Football League was wonderful and there are so many tales I could tell you. One in particular springs to mind...

We had a fixture up at Halifax Town and the referee was having a poor game (as is often the case when you're playing away from home). I was in the directors' box next to Jim and he was so upset I'm sure I could see steam coming out of his ears. He kept standing up and shouting at the ref – which is banned in directors' boxes in the Football League – and an official arrived and sternly warned Jim about his behaviour.

Just as Jim was being cautioned, another seemingly biased decision went Halifax's way. Absolutely fuming he leapt out of his seat, brushed past the steward and scooted down the steps of the stand to give the ref what-for, but running too fast he hit the protective rail at waist height and span over the barrier, falling ten feet onto the spectators below.

When I got to the bottom of the steps I didn't know what to expect but there was dear old Jim, picking himself up and the five other people he'd fallen on. It was a miracle no one was badly hurt. Jim didn't return to the directors' box.

At each club I've been involved with I've always had a degree of input when it came to negotiating transfer fees and at Maidstone Jim left that side of the business to me. I remember taking a call one Friday afternoon from First Division Wimbledon, who were offering £100,000 for our winsome defender Warren Barton. I told their manager Bobby

Gould that I needed time to consult with the chairman who was out having his usual long lunch.

I tracked down Jim in a restaurant and he said the offer sounded good but to wait until he returned to the office before accepting it. As I put down the phone Bobby rang again to say he had heard that Warren was going to Liverpool for talks so he would improve the offer to £200,000 if I said yes there and then. I told Bobby that the lad was going nowhere and that I had to wait to run the offer past the boss. Ten minutes later Jim returned from his lunch and agreed the sale at £200,000 as we were in a financial stew at the time and needed the money. Then Bobby phoned again but before I could accept his offer, he said the Wimbledon chairman Sam Hamman was sitting beside him and he wanted the player so badly he would increase the bid to £300,000 – the largest sum paid for a Fourth Division player at the time – on the basis that there would be no on-going payments. We agreed and Jim congratulated me on being such a good negotiator, but it was the easiest hand of football poker I had ever played.

Warren was a huge asset to the side so when he was sold it felt like the club had begun the slide into a serious financial crisis. Soon after we suffered another bitter blow, when permission to develop forty-five acres of land at Hollingbourne the club had bought for £400,000 into a £25 million leisure complex promising something for everyone – a cinema, function suite, bowling alley, railway station, cattle market and 10,000-seater stadium – was denied by the council.

Keith Peacock and his assistant Tommy Taylor had also been losing their way, so the board decided it was time for a change and Graham Carr – father of comedian Alan Carr – was installed as the new boss. With him came an assistant, Clive Walker (not to be confused with the former Chelsea star).

The training methods changed dramatically overnight which didn't go down well with the players: running up and down hills was now the order of the day and the football switched to a long-ball approach. Meanwhile crowds were plummeting (average gates dropped from 2,427 to 1,429 between 1989 and 1992) results got worse, money was in short supply and we still couldn't find a way back home. There were a lot of furrowed brows around the office at the time and I could sense the same bad vibes that I had experienced at Sacramento Gold.

With big trouble on the horizon Jim decided to sack Graham Carr following more bad results and although Clive Walker was kept on to train the team, I was called in and asked to act as caretaker manager until Jim found someone else. 'You're the only one who understands the dressing room,' he pleaded.

Although I say it myself it wasn't the correct appointment but I had always dreamed of being a Football League manager so I agreed, saying to myself that if I was going to do it, I was going to do it right.

Now, when an Old Sod (or 'General Manager' to use my actual job title at the time) is introduced to a team in this manner and under these circumstances, I can tell you that you are certainly not welcomed with open arms. Indeed, the first couple of weeks were very difficult as I introduced a regime of fitness and team work in the morning, a light lunch, then tactics and set-plays in the afternoon. That went down like a lead balloon as the players were used to having the afternoons to themselves.

My first game in charge during the 1991/1992 season was away to Scunthorpe. We lost 2-0 so there was more fitness training and tactical work the following week, even though the addition of afternoon sessions was still causing me a great deal of grief.

My second game was away at Mansfield. Needless to say it was important for us to stop the rot and I obviously wanted to do well against my old club. Before kick-off I had a word with Smokey and Liburd Henry – our two quickest forwards – and asked them to sit high up the field early on and virtually mark their two sluggish centre-backs. But twenty minutes into the game, neither had done as I'd asked and we were two-nil down.

It was not the first time in my management career that I got the distinct impression the players were ignoring what I had said, so I decided to let everyone know who was calling the shots: I don't think I'd ever made a double substitution before – certainly not after twenty-five minutes – and both strikers slunk past me on their way to the dressing rooms.

After the game (which we lost) I was so cross I told the players they had fifteen minutes to shower and ten minutes to have a drink and that anyone who was not on the coach by exactly ten past five could make their own way home.

When the driver pulled out of the Field Mill gates there was plenty of room on board, as his trio of passengers – midfielder Gary Stebbing, physio Frank Brooks and yours truly – couldn't help but notice. I have to admit that my conscience pricked on the way home and I prepared myself for the fallout the following Monday, while hoping that after a row there would be greater respect for the new gaffer and his methods.

The barney between myself the players was just as vociferous as I had expected, but I felt the air was now clear and we could move on to the next game – Cardiff away. We knew the gate was expected to be around 15,000 as the club was opening a new stand.

On the coach home – which this time was fairly full! – I spent most of the journey pinching myself after a scoreline of Cardiff City 0, Maidstone United 5. It was a magnificent result, a great performance and for a moment I believed that we were turning our albeit sinking ship towards shallower waters.

That thin ray of hope faded fast as back at the office bad news was flooding in: bills were not being paid, takeover rumours were rife and the press was full of gossip. I was then hit with the biggest body blow in all my time in football and as you've already read, I'd taken a few punches for my teams over the years.

Jim called me in and said that although he had tried everything in his power to keep the club afloat, his last hope was to strike some half-arsed deal with a businessman called John Waugh, who wanted to buy Maidstone United, transplant it to the north-east, merge it with a non-league club called Newcastle Blue Star and call it Newcastle Browns. Jim added that while he was very sorry, there had to be casualties and he could no longer afford to keep me.

In short, I had to go.

13

The Enemy Within

WHEN I rejoined Maidstone United in 1981 the directors
gave me a crystal-clear brief that never changed over
the following years: you get the team into the Football League
and we will supply a new stadium (he-he-he).

I do believe – and always will – that Jim Thompson did just
about everything to keep the club alive: after all, Maidstone
United was his life. The only question that ever crossed my
mind was: were the finances managed correctly? We can only
guess the answer to that.

I was in such a state in the weeks following my sacking
that I can't recall much of what happened around that time.
What I do know is that going home to tell your family that you
are out of work and have no idea what is coming next is not a
very pleasant thing to do.

However, Jim phoned me a few weeks later to pass on a
whisper that Gillingham were interested in hiring me as their

general and commercial manager. 'You've got to be joking,' I said. 'I can't see that happening; I'd be the enemy within!'

After all, it hadn't been *that* many months since my beloved Maidstone United had beaten Gillingham at Priestfield (2-1, Butler, Gall) in the Fourth Division on Boxing Day 1989. And it hadn't been *that* many weeks since Maidstone United had beaten Gillingham at Priestfield (1-0, Lillis) to win the Kent Senior Cup in May 1990. And it hadn't been *that* many days since Maidstone United had beaten Gillingham at Priestfield (2-0, Pritchard, Osbourne) in the League again the following September. Mind you, I suppose it had been a few years now since Frank Ovard curled that chip over Ron Hillyard's curly mullet at the Town End to crown Mark Newson's opener, when Maidstone United beat Gillingham at Priestfield for a place in the Third Round of the FA Cup, three days before the Christmas of 1980.

Obviously I didn't need to whip off my shirt and reveal my tattoo of Winstone (remember him?) for Jim to know exactly where my club colours lay. But he kindly reminded me that I had no work, no money and no prospects, adding that if he was in my shoes he would take the job. He also said that if I did decide to accept the position, I could go to Gillingham with Maidstone's thanks and blessings.

Blessings my arse! When I took the job the local press ran splashes along the lines of *RAT LEAVES SINKING SHIP* and there was not a single supportive quote from the club. I have always hoped that report was written without consultation with Jim. I certainly know that no one contacted me.

The 1992/1993 season saw the old First Division change to the Premier League and the Second became the First and so on. Maidstone were therefore due to be founder members of the new Third Division, but as the campaign drew nearer it seemed increasingly likely that they would not be able to play in the League as the club was poorer than a church mouse in a double-dip recession.

The Stones were due to play their opening game of the season away at Scunthorpe United on 15 August, 1992. Unfortunately, come the date, the club had the same number of players on their books as they had pound coins in the bank – two – so unable to honour their fixtures they were forced to resign from the League and went into liquidation.

To state the obvious it was a massively miserable day when it became clear that Maidstone United had ceased to exist. Many hundreds were left devastated and wondering what they were going to do on Saturday afternoons.

Charlton Athletic were the first vultures to come circling and immediately offered discounted coach and ticket packages to whisk many of our supporters up to The Valley. It was simple commercialism of course, but I thought their timing was nothing short of brutal.

Whatever, after a couple of meetings with Gillingham chairman Bernard Baker and owner Tony Smith, I agreed to start work immediately. They made it clear they wanted me to build the club's commercial portfolio and bring in some much-needed revenue.

Pitching up at Gillingham wasn't the problem I had

envisaged: in fact I was welcomed back with open arms as many of the club's older supporters remembered my four-and-a-half years there as skipper and regarded me as someone who always gave one hundred per cent.

But my football life had changed completely: after so many years running the team I now had no input whatsoever and I missed creating good football players and building winning sides. Mind you, as I make these comments now, I'm not sure whether at the time I was disappointed or relieved: years of trying to help football teams win matches takes its toll on the mind and body, as anyone that knows me well will confirm.

Gillingham's owner Tony Smith was a lovely man. He'd made a lot of money from the sale of Wards estate agents and his wife Val was lovely too. She came from the Hales footballing dynasty and her brother, Derek, was the Charlton legend who infamously threw the first punch in the on-field scrap with strike partner Mike Flanagan during Maidstone United's FA Cup Third Round tie at The Valley in January 1979.

That incident is etched on the memory of many Stones fans: with five minutes to go and the game level at 1-1, Flanagan played the ball through to Hales. Hales was ruled offside and was furious as he'd wanted the ball played a lot earlier. Flanagan, who had scored Charlton's equaliser minutes earlier, said – using slightly different words to these – that he'd been doing that all season but Hales hadn't been taking advantage. They began brawling and were sent off by referee Brian Martin.

It was clear during my first conducted tour of Priestfield for more than twenty years that the stadium was falling apart and needed a huge injection of cash. Unfortunately there was no budget for that. Damien Richardson's players, meanwhile, were seemingly inept: I think that during the 1992/1993 season the goalkeeper managed to get himself sent off three times before Christmas, the team conceded injury-time goals in four consecutive away games and, to cap it all, over ten mad days in March, they netted no fewer than *five* own goals.

Off the pitch a massive commercial drive swung into action to address some of the club's shortfalls. My new-fashioned match days felt strange at first, largely because making sure there was enough tea and coffee in the hospitality areas seemed more important than Nicky Forster nicking the team a winner.

My assistant at Priestfield was a lad named Mike Ling and he was great company. We would usually travel to away games together: we'd get there early, have a meal, watch the game and then come home. No pressure. Simple.

I remember the team had an FA Cup tie away at Huddersfield. Mike was unable to make it so our printer, Tommy Fogarty, invited me to travel with him, along with his business partner Allen Trice and a huge bouncer mate of Tommy's who'd been hired as our chauffeur.

It grew increasingly icy on the way to West Yorkshire and snow began to fall, but we made it to our hotel and happily drained a few glasses over lunch. Thankfully the game hadn't been called off and at the ground I hooked up with an old friend, the former Republic of Ireland and Huddersfield manager Eoin Hand. During the match Eoin told me that he owned a nightclub in the town and wanted to invite the four of us to join him there after the game which, somewhat irrelevantly, we lost.

Gratefully we accepted and after spending a couple of hours enjoying a few drinks at the bar, we found ourselves precariously near the dance floor. Now, I had heard about 'Grab a Granny' nights before, but when I noticed the coachload of mature ladies drinking steadily at the surrounding tables, I realised that I was now slap bang in the middle of one.

I had no time to think. Suddenly the DJ cranked up the volume and the walls were swaying to *Stayin' Alive*. Needing no invitation – let alone a warm-up – Little Tommy, who was no taller than five-foot five, and The Big Bouncer Bloke, who was no shorter than six-foot six, broke into a better synchronised *Saturday Night Fever* dance routine than you'll ever see on *Strictly Come Dancing*.

Quick as a flash, a disco inferno spread through the nightclub like wildfire. The gaggle of old birds were well up for a laugh after sinking a few port and lemons, so they slipped into their Dr Scholl's, eased to their feet and began copying every move that Tommy and the big fella made. It was hilarious – one of those special moments in life – and everyone in the club was in stitches.

It was the small hours when we staggered out into the cold. There were no taxis around so hugging the wheel of Tommy's top-of-the-range Jaguar, the bouncer began to 'drive' us back to the hotel. By now there was a blizzard blowing and we were still in gales of laughter; so much so we failed to notice the string of parked cars that the bouncer was smashing the Jag into.

We certainly weren't laughing the next morning: the offside of the car was perfect but the nearside looked as though a tank had run down its flank. Tommy wasn't particularly amused, understandably, but it had been a damn good night. Mind you, I do wish I could remember the name of that flaming bouncer...

My job at Gillingham was going well and there was much to do. I launched a new lottery called Superloot and Mike Ling and I signed up more than a hundred newsagents and recruited a couple of thousand members by knocking on doors: the buzz I had felt while selling in South Africa had returned.

However, results on the Priestfield pitch were so poor that in the autumn of 1992, Damien and his assistant Ron Hillyard were sacked and Glenn Roeder drafted in.

The club remained on the rocks for the rest of the season and relegation to the Conference was a distinct possibility: The Gills went into the final game of the season needing to beat Halifax to stay up, which they managed with a nervy 2-0 win.

Even though they avoided the drop I know for a fact that in Gillingham's corridors of power at the end of the 1992/1993 season, plans were afoot to get Glenn Roeder out of the door by hook or by crook. But when Watford made a surprise move for him, he naffed off under his own steam. Consequently,

Watford were fined £10,000 for the illegal approach and Gillingham were compensated to the tune of £30,000 – what a result!

With Roeder gone his assistant, Mike Flanagan, was appointed to ensure the club's survival, but the financial crisis continued and steadily improving league form over the following two seasons did little to disguise the fact that the club was in real danger of folding.

Gillingham FC eventually went into receivership in January 1995. The chief executive at the time was Barry Bright – now chairman of the FA's Disciplinary Committee – and over a beer in the Priestfield Club he tipped me the wink that we could all be out of work within hours.

He wasn't wrong. The next day the administrators called us all in and, in my case, I was given two hours to clear my desk and hand over my keys. After a few choice words to anyone within earshot I drove home to tell Jill. Here we go again, I thought to myself. And what on Earth was I going to put on my CV? What was my job? What business was I actually in? I had nothing lined up this time. More importantly, I felt I was no longer in demand.

14

Hi-de-Hi, Lo-di-Lo

OUT of work and with wolves knocking at my door (shame it wasn't Wolves really), I reluctantly made my debut appearance in the dole queue at the grand old age of fifty-two.

If you've never needed to claim unemployment benefit, lucky you, as in my case I found it to be a most degrading experience. Signing on is unavoidable in most cases but you have my word that lining up behind other jobless souls is not so good for your self-esteem.

It was indeed a very low point in my life: the double whammy of the Maidstone and Gillingham collapses made me feel as though twelve years of my time had been wasted. It probably wasn't a very sensible thing to do but I remember working out the exact number of hours I had invested over those dozen years and, believe it or not, it reached a ridiculous figure; something like 35,000. And here I was with nothing to show for it. Who was to blame?

I know people don't tend to lose their money on purpose but it has always amazed me why businessmen with proven business backgrounds are not able to apply good practice and live within their means when they take on a football club. Bitterness is a very heavy sack to carry but it never weighs me down for long.

Happily, some joyous news back at Williams' Towers kept the family smiling: we had known for nine months that Samantha was expecting a child and bang on time – 27 September 1995 – our beautiful first grandchild, Emily Claire Williams, entered the world.

After six weeks of popping into Maidstone to sign on (not that I was getting any money) I took a call from Tony Smith at Gillingham. He thanked me for all I had done for the club and offered me some redundancy cash: I knew it came from him personally and I shall always be grateful as it helped the family through a difficult time. Tony was a good guy.

Then, soon after, I was invited to a meeting with Gillingham's former chairman, Bernard Baker, who apparently had a proposal he thought may interest me. 'I'm putting together a consortium to buy Cardiff City' was his opening line and he wanted me, plus his business partner, his solicitor and the company accountant to travel to Wales the following week to discuss the deal with Cardiff's owner Rick Wright.

We sat with Mr Wright in the John Charles Suite overlooking Ninian Park and outside it was sheeting with rain. Rick, an Australian impresario who owned companies around the world, was an interesting man but very abrupt.

'You can have the club for a million,' he said. 'Look at the books. I'll give you three weeks to get the money if you're interested. Speak to anyone; you have my permission.' Then he left.

After chewing it over it was agreed that the accountant and I would spend the next fortnight carrying out a complete financial and commercial audit, which was a reasonably simple exercise as the club was well organised and every scrap of the company was registered somewhere.

But what we failed to fully take on board was the strength of support that underpins Cardiff City, and as soon as word was out that a consortium was in town people appeared from every nook and cranny wanting to meet with us.

To quell their fears, our commercial manager popped over from Swansea and presented a stunning commercial proposition which made us feel a lot more bullish about moving the deal forward. Our only real concern was over the ugly arm of Cardiff's fan base: the club had earned itself a reputation for bad behaviour and we wondered if the naughty boys would rail against the family approach that we were proposing to bring to The Valleys.

We therefore arranged a meeting with a group of the club's hardcore fans and more than two hundred turned up to listen to our ideas. The event was very constructive until the moment our accountants described the supporters' bar – in which we were sitting at the time – as 'outdated', adding that the best thing was for it to disappear in a puff of smoke. They didn't mean it literally, of course, and I'm sure the naughty boys were probably not to blame, probably, but one night the following week the clubhouse easily came off second best against a can of petrol and a box of Swan Vesta.

After many days spent in Wales we were ready to submit our bid to Rick Wright. He decided he wanted to amend a couple of points so the discussions were protracted for a further three weeks. Eventually Rick said he was ready but had just one more person to speak with, so we happily returned to Kent convinced we had bought Cardiff City. Two days later Rick phoned to say our bid had been gazumped by the notorious Kumar brothers from Birmingham.

I was still licking my wounds and contemplating what owning Cardiff City would have felt like compared to living on the rock 'n' roll, when Rick Wright phoned again. He apologised that we had lost out on City and wanted to offer us an alternative business deal to make up. So it was off to Cardiff once again, where Rick explained that he was planning to sell all of his remaining UK assets and return to his native Australia to breed trotting ponies.

'How would you like to run a holiday camp?' he asked, explaining how he needed to flog the former Butlins site he owned on Barry Island.

Spread over fifty-seven acres it had eight hundred chalets, four swimming pools, a 2000-seater theatre, two ballrooms, three night clubs and the obligatory boulevard of shops. It supported thirty-five permanent staff, more than a hundred part-timers and hired twenty entertainers each week. The consortium decided it was interested in the proposition so

Wearing the face of a man who can't believe what he's just done,
Steve Galloway turns the Watford faithful to stone and sparks
an incredible scoreboard at Vicarage Road, January 1987.

Fourth Division here we come: celebrating at Runcorn as Conference champions, 1989.

Jim and I join the party while Steve Butler checks his phone bill.

Sharing a joke with Manchester United and England legend Nobby Stiles during a Maidstone United Sporting Dinner at the Great Danes Hotel.

What a lovely day Jill and I spent with Sir Alex at Old Trafford.

Why is there a photo of Des Lynam in my book? [Editor's note: It's you Bill, in 2000.]

My lovely Aunt Enid, bless her.

Our beloved Claire, always in our hearts.

Team Williams pushes goal-line technology to its limit, 2012. From left: Emily, Catherine, James, Jill, me, Samantha, Nick and Elizabeth.

once again our 'due-diligence' gang swung into action and back to Cardiff we went.

Rick invited us to stay at his house while we made up our minds. He lived in a glorious stately home that had five en-suite bedrooms, two huge reception rooms, a snooker room and the longest drive I have ever driven up. Oh, and there was a cook and a housekeeper and it overlooked the sea.

From the house to the holiday camp was the most beautiful walk around the headland of Nell's Point and the views over the folding waves were simply stunning. Rick explained that if we bought the holiday camp, this fabulous accommodation would be included as part of the package. Hi-de-bloody-hi, I thought to myself.

We were eyeing up the site in the close season and looking through some old diaries I am reminded that we eventually took control in January 1995. We must have therefore been going through the books and weighing up the possibilities during the previous October and November, which rings true as I will never forget that Barry Island is bloody freezing in winter. Regardless, after much deliberation, the consortium completed the deal and when the responsibilities were divvied up, I was appointed General Manager.

And there was so much for me to crack on with: the site had some excellent entertainment spaces but also some very downtrodden areas that were in a shocking state of disrepair. Indeed, under Rick Wright's ownership, the camp had been the subject of an investigation by the BBC consumer programme *That's Life*, which makes for an interesting little tale...

Following complaints about the condition of the site, the show's flamboyant journalist-come-musician, Doc Cox, paid a visit and after finding some litter and a few black bin bags sang, to the tune of *I Do Like To Be Beside The Seaside*, a most unflattering ditty entitled *It's Barry Awful, It's Barry Hell.*

At the end of the report presenter Esther Rantzen asked those viewers who were off to Barry Island that year if they would send a postcard to the studio reviewing their holiday. Well, believe it or not, Rick had thousands of pre-paid postcards printed and asked everyone he knew to send a fistful into the programme. As such, *That's Life* received more than 8000 postcards praising the camp and only forty-odd complaints. The BBC was forced to issue an apology and Rick sued them, bagging half-a-million quid in damages.

Considering the poor overall state of the site, my first job was to hire a team of designers to devise some fresh ideas for the various sections and also appoint a marketing company to promote the business.

In no time at all, we re-branded the camp the 'Barry Island Resort' and the site became a hive of activity as we set in motion a plan to revitalise the entire fifty-seven acres. This obviously had to be done in stages, so we started on the first two-hundred chalets, then the theatre, the shopping parade and the huge Pig and Whistle entertainment bar. In addition to the existing staff, more than two hundred part-timers were employed in preparation for the new season.

Our resident group was twelve-piece function ensemble

The John Oliver Band, and to say they were brilliant would be an understatement. John came to see me one afternoon and suggested that to put the island on the map (I quickly reminded him it was now a 'resort'), we needed to book some headline acts. The idea was that if we could attract household names to perform, not only would we draw a bevy of holidaymakers but we could also open the doors to the locals once a week.

I can still remember the first three acts that we booked; Freddie and the Dreamers, Gerry and the Pacemakers and The Commitments. As I had grown up with their music, it was a wonderful step back in time and having played guitar for the past thirty years, I relished the chance to climb on stage and jam with some of my musical heroes.

However, although I was the paymaster, I soon realised that all of the bands' musicians were totally out of my league and I just couldn't face up to the potential embarrassment. Sadly, then, my guitar stayed tucked up in its case.

We had many great nights in the Barry Island ballroom with performances by some of the world's biggest names. In particular, I won't forget when The Stylistics topped the bill...

Earlier in the day I'd taken a call from the secretary of Kent County Cricket Club, who asked if it would be possible for a couple of the players to come down for the evening as their match against Glamorgan had been rained off. That was no problem at all as the pair of lads in question – wicket-keeper Steve Marsh and fast bowler Martin McCague – were old drinking pals of mine from a Kent pub in the middle of nowhere called the Who'd A Thought It (otherwise known by some lost souls as the Who Can Find It).

Steve and Martin pitched up in time for the supporting acts and soon began tucking into the beer. That was nothing new: according to Steve's autobiography, Martin sank seventy-two pints of Guinness on a stag weekend in Dublin.

I must admit that I did stitch the lads up that night, and on the pretence of a behind-the-scenes tour, I shoved them on stage to push pineapples and shake a tree as Black Lace ploughed through their novelty hit *Agadoo*.

Three hours, a dozen pints and several Scotches later, the place was rocking and I noticed for the first time that with a couple of thousand bodies boogying to the music, the dance floor literally bounced up and down to the tune of six inches.

The ballroom had a massive bar at each end and the dance area was surrounded by three tiers, above which was a low balcony where we had an area roped off for special guests. Anyway, now more leathered than a pair of cricket balls, Steve and Martin were spinning around having a wonderful time when all of a sudden their feet disappeared over the balcony and they both splashed ten feet down onto a table of holidaymakers from Up North. Broken glass was flying all over the place and the lads were so lucky they weren't badly hurt. And thank heavens there was no cricket the next day.

Talking of holidaymakers from the North, it was a fact that the majority of our visitors came from Sheffield, Manchester and Liverpool. Most of the guests were fun-loving and just looking for a really good break from their normal lives, but we did have a number of Families From Hell and, on reflection, I'm sure we would have made a few bob if we'd filmed a fly-on-the-wall documentary series at the site.

To keep the peace, we employed thirty-five bouncers ('doormen' today) from South Glamorgan Security, and they acted as the Barry Island Resort Police Force. They were absolutely brilliant and helped create a friendly and trouble-free environment. Certainly, when the nightclubs turned out in the early hours, the security boys earned their money by making sure that everyone got home safely and, ideally, to their own chalet. Their night shift finished at eight in the morning but often there would still be bodies lying around in the different buildings when it was time for them to call it a night.

As you will gather my new job was a sea-change for me, so much so that if I had been asked before I took the role whether or not I would be able to adapt to it, I would certainly have answered 'no'. But after nine months everything was going swimmingly and I was loving every minute of it – there was so much variation and no two days were the same.

The company I was working for had major plans and the main reason for taking on the camp in the first place was to gain access to the local waterfronts, which were prime sites where a housing complex and marinas could be created.

The majority of the management team were working sixty hours a week and negotiations had started with the Local Government Group to convert some of the site into factory storage areas and at the same time buy up the waterfront.

Everything was ticking along nicely until the local council

stepped in to confirm that there was no chance of us gaining further planning permission or obtaining a change of use. Simultaneously, those lovely boys at Health and Safety issued a restraining notice on our existing fire alarm and sprinkler system, adding that new equipment would need to be installed at an estimated cost of – wait for it – £850,000.

Such work could wait until winter, though, so to bring down the curtain on the summer season, we staged a festival of rock and roll music over a weekend in September. We invited twenty-four bands to play and that week's headliners were also still at the camp. And what a great time we had: the crowds were immense and I recall that we took more than £80,000 over the bar alone.

However, on the Monday morning after the weekend before, I was woken at early o'clock by an urgent telephone call from one of the security guards, who wanted me to jump out of bed and get down to the resort as quickly as possible.

'Have you been in the vaults and banked the cash?' he asked. I told him I hadn't as Bernard Baker, the owner of the company, had taken the safe key the previous evening saying he would bank the returns. That was not unusual; it had happened plenty of times before. What was unusual though, was that Bernard and the cash were nowhere to be found. Also on the missing list was the balance of the company's two bank accounts, the contents of the boss's office, the firm's Rolls-Royce and, believe it or not, the female singer from The John Oliver Band.

Lo-di-bloody-lo, I thought to myself.

15

Coast to Coast

WITH the runaway owner of the Barry Island Resort
now holding all of the company's worldly goods firmly
in his hands, along with, presumably, the pair of assets
belonging to a certain female vocalist, the police were called
and an emergency board meeting convened.

It definitely didn't take our accountant many minutes to
confirm that every penny had been filched from the company
and it didn't take the police much longer to work out that they
were dealing with a rather serious case of theft. This was, of
course, not the first time I had faced a similar picture to the
one that had just been painted, so my gut feeling was to jump
into my car and head for the hills. However, I felt that morally
someone should stick around to front the legions of upset staff
and suppliers while at the same time consider if there was
any possibility that a rescue package could be launched.

I did everything I could to find fresh investment but

following the council's statement about the lease, no one wanted to know. Many people's lives were affected by Bernard hightailing and by far the hardest part for me was breaking the news to those who had worked at the camp all their lives. The expression on their faces almost slaughtered me.

It's amazing what comes to light when something so dramatic happens. It turned out that Bernard thought he was merely grabbing back some of his initial investment. But he had obviously been planning his great escape for some time and it soon became clear that our suppliers had not been paid for at least three months. With no one else to blame, the creditors began gunning for the general manager and I found myself on the receiving end of several nasty threats.

The sharpest of the knives that were out for me was held by the local butcher. He was owed thousands of pounds and one morning he burst past security and smashed through my office door wielding a tasty-looking meat cleaver. 'What are you going to do with that?' I asked.

'Get some of my money back.'

'All the money's gone,' I explained.

'Find some.'

'You can have the forty quid I've got in my pocket.'

'F*** off!' he blasted, 'I'd rather chop you into little pieces!'

As you can imagine, I didn't really know what to say after that, but I managed to calm him down and the confrontation thankfully ended without me looking like I had just staggered out of an episode of *Hammer House of Horror*.

Needless to say it wasn't a great start to the day but

things got even worse later that afternoon when I had my final meeting with the head of South Glamorgan Security. Unsurprisingly, they were also out of pocket, in their case to the tune of £45,000.

The security boss was understandably very angry and regarded me as partly responsible for the debacle, but I had got on well with him in the past and when I explained what had happened he agreed to accept a promissory note from me. It was something I knew I could never honour (years later, incidentally, the debt between us was written off) but I could see no way of getting out of the place in one piece without offering such an assurance.

I can still recall my overwhelming feeling of relief as I drove out of the gates of the Barry Island Resort for the last time. That said, my departure was soaked in sadness, largely due to the way our experience in Wales had smashed into the buffers. Still, over the years Jill and I had grown accustomed to dealing with sudden and wholesale changes in our life.

Bearing in mind that the family had recently agreed to buy a house in Penarth and arranged for James to attend the local school, I guess we were a lucky as we fortunately just managed to dodge those commitments. But what now lay in store for the Williams family; what was out there waiting for us?

Well, in December 1996, I took a call from the chairman of Conference side Dover Athletic, John Husk, who wanted to know if I would consider a return to football by becoming their manager. My old friend Peter Taylor had been in charge during the 1995/1996 season and had signed a two-year contract in the May. However, during the summer he received an offer from England boss Glenn Hoddle to run the England Under 21 side which, understandably, Peter didn't want to turn down. Former Chelmsford City boss Joe O'Sullivan then took the reins of the troubled club for the start of the 1996/1997 season, but he had recently resigned, apparently after being spat at by supporters following a run of rubbish results.

The Whites were bottom of the league when I was invited for an interview. It was held at one of the director's houses and there must have been at least fifteen committee members waiting to grill me: I'm not sure if the kit man was there as well, but in hindsight he may just as well have been. The interview went well and a couple of days later I was offered a full-time job running both the first team and the commercial operation. That was no problem for me, of course, as I was well qualified on both fronts.

What was a problem, though, was that in the few hours between the interview and my appointment, the board of directors had taken it upon themselves to sell the club's leading goal scorer, David Leworthy, to our nearest relegation rivals Rushden & Diamonds for £12,500. Now that may sound like a fair deal, but the intelligent striker had been bought by Dover from Farnborough Town three years earlier for a non-league transfer fee record of, believe it or not, £50,000. Moreover, as he'd been bagging thirty goals a season, I regarded David as our salvation to keep the club in the Conference.

When I pointed this out to the board their answer was

alarming: 'We didn't think we had much of chance of staying in the league and we really needed the cash.' Unbelievable.

On the plus side, Dover had a decent regular income as they ran one of the most successful lotteries outside of the Football League. Before the launch of the National Lottery three years earlier in 1994, they were netting around £6,000 a week and although the advent of the state-franchised big-prize raffle had slashed the club's income in half, £3,000 gave me a decent budget for players and, of course, I had no intention of seeing my side relegated.

The team I inherited from Peter – via Joe – was as poor as any I had come across in my career. It even crossed my mind that The John Oliver Band could have fielded a stronger eleven. The squad therefore needed a major overhaul but as it was now January, there really wasn't enough time left in the season for that. However, I quickly added five league players and dumped a few out. Clive Walker joined me as coach and the team immediately began picking up points.

For my first game in charge, top-of-the-table Macclesfield Town pitched up at The Crabble. Their manager was former Manchester United midfielder Sammy McIlroy who had, the previous season, guided Macclesfield to the Conference title (although they were denied promotion to the Football League as their Moss Rose ground did not have enough seats). Sammy was in a bubbly mood before the game and was no doubt expecting his side to be heading back up the M1 later in the day with three easy points. However, an incredible long-range strike by Steve Brown and a winner from Gary Stebbing earned us a marvellous 2-1 victory. Sammy, needless to say, wasn't quite so sunny after the game.

It was just the result we needed to give everyone enough confidence to imagine that we could stay in the league. And fight off relegation we jolly well did, which was a huge feat under the circumstances and set a solid platform for the following season's campaign.

When you arrive at a club as the new manager, you always need to make small tweaks to ensure that the job can be done smoothly, and I immediately saw something that seemed a little cock-eyed during Dover's away fixtures.

Anyone who has played for or supported a team in the Conference will know that the amount of travelling involved can be ridiculous and Dover, of course, always had that extra few miles to trek. My first couple of away games were a unique experience because for the first time there were two or three ladies travelling with the team. Now, I'm certainly not a male chauvinist (am I Jill?) but across all the years I had been in football and over all the miles I had spent on coaches, I had never travelled with ladies on board. Cue my first run-in with the chairman.

'Those three women have done more for this club than anyone else on board,' he said, 'and they will be travelling with team every week.'

The streak of Clough in me was tempted to suggest that if that was to be the case, then he could stick his job where the sun doesn't shine. However, the Paisley part of me came up with a deal.

'If I agree that the ladies can travel on the bus, will you let me sign a player or two when I need them?' I suggested.

The chairman shook on the deal and during the next year I added a few more players to the squad. As such, my first full season at Dover ended with the club in thirteenth position and I felt we were in a decent position to attack the league the following year.

Mind you, the 1997/1998 season produced my biggest footballing disappointment for many years.

As you've read, I played eight times for England Under 18s and spent time at some reasonable clubs but, like so many other professional players, I had never enjoyed the experience of walking out at Wembley. Although I had obviously hung up my boots many moons earlier, the twin towers were now in sight as Dover Athletic had fought their way to the quarter-finals of the FA Trophy.

We faced Barrow at The Crabble but could only manage a 1-1 draw, which left us with a mammoth schlep to Cumbria on the Tuesday for the replay. The scores were level after ninety minutes and then still level after extra time, so the boys loaded their boots for a penalty shootout. We hit all five and won 5-4. We got home at four in the morning by which time I was convinced our name was on the cup.

I know that there are many Dover supporters who are still haunted by the two-legged semi-final against Cheltenham Town. In the first match, at their place, we lost 2-1 to a pair of dodgy goals (the ball had gone out of play during the build-up to their first and the second was such a clear-cut case of handball that even if the referee was Blind Pew he would have blown his whistle).

Although we had been beaten over in Gloucestershire, I was still convinced we could turn Cheltenham over at The Crabble and begin planning our big day out at Wembley. We were dreadful, though, again losing 2-1 – so 4-2 on aggregate – and the dream was gone; this time forever.

Meanwhile, much to our surprise, Jill and I had discovered that another Baby Williams would soon be making its debut appearance, and on 2 August 1998, Samantha gave birth to a second lovely daughter, Catherine Jane. (This is all well and good, I said to myself, but how are we going to keep the family name going at this rate? I really was hoping for a prospective skipper for the first team!)

Despite the disappointment of our Trophy exit Dover played some decent football during the 1998/1999 season and finished in eleventh spot. We therefore had a strong squad in place for the start of the 1999/2000 campaign.

Our first game was away at Kidderminster who, in the close season, had landed a high-profile new manager in the form of ex-Liverpool star Jan Molby. Just prior to accepting the position with The Harriers, the great Dane had been approached by tiny Welsh League side Rhayader, who at the time were seriously strapped for cash and fighting relegation. Amusingly, they had made a rather cheeky bid to the beefy midfielder, by offering to pay him for his playing skills not in money but, believe it or not, in meat. Speaking to the

Daily Mirror, Rhayader club secretary – my old mucker Phil Woosnam – had insisted that the offer was certainly not a publicity stunt as many of the Rhayader committee members were farmers so they could literally pay him in steaks.

Anyway, the arrival of Molby, whose thick Scouse accent had become familiar to football fans thanks to his punditry on BBC Radio 5 Live, caused quite a buzz around the ground and I could feel waves of expectation spilling down the terraces. The crowd was not disappointed: we thoroughly played them off the park and won the match 2-1. The scoreline flattered them – we should have scored six and it was clearly no fluke.

From that superb start we went on a run of eighteen games unbeaten, which took us to the top of the Conference. Naturally, I could see the Football League on the horizon...

However, in the February we played second placed Rushden & Diamonds at home. More than four thousand turned up at The Crabble and bearing in mind we had not been beaten for several months, our tails were up. That counted for nothing though, as we found ourselves on the end of a 4-0 thumping and to this day I still cannot put my finger on what went so horribly wrong.

But what did go horribly wrong the following Monday morning was quite transparent: John Husk called me in and explained that because the club was in debt he would need to sell some of the players to keep the bank off his back.

John was a first-class chairman and a first-class man and I had never had a problem with him, but this news was the last thing I wanted to hear and I made my feelings quite clear to him. Nevertheless, he won the argument and we sold Ricky Reina to Brentford for £50,000, Simon Wormull to Rushden for another £50,000, Charlie Mitten to Gillingham for £18,000 and Joe Dunne to Colchester for £15,000. Those deals made Mr NatWest very happy. Meanwhile, John was very sad, I was steaming and the fans were revolting.

We ended the season in sixth position and although it was the club's highest ever league finish, it was little consolation as I firmly believed that without having to strip the squad of quality players, I could well have led Dover Athletic into the Football League.

16

Williams Out!

THE shedding of the squad signalled the beginning of the end for me on the south coast. But I was not the only one whose days were numbered at Dover Athletic: when the severity of the club's financial difficulties became common knowledge – they were in hock by more than £100,000 – John Husk resigned as chairman. The new board then made it clear that they were looking for a younger man to manage the side and thanked me for the wonderful job I had done at the club over the previous four years.

As soon as the news broke I was approached with a couple of offers, the most interesting of which was to join Kingstonian as their team and commercial manager. The three-year deal that was on the table was outstanding – in fact I thought I had won the Lottery! – so in August 2001, off I went to fresh fields.

The previous season Kingstonian had struggled financially and suffered relegation from the Conference. As such, they parted company with their legendary manager, Geoff Chapple, who had led them to the Isthmian League title in 1998 and then back-to-back FA Trophy wins at Wembley in 1999 and 2000.

Earlier in 2001, Geoff had very nearly taken the team to the Fifth Round of the FA Cup after beating two Football League clubs – Brentford 3-1 away in the First Round and Southend United 1-0 away in the Third Round. They had then been seconds away from overcoming Bristol City in the Fourth Round before succumbing to a late winner in the replay. The renowned manager had earlier in his career also won the FA Trophy three times with Woking Town (1994, 1995 and 1997) so, to put it mildly, Geoff was going to be a hard act to follow.

The first board meeting I attended at Kingstonian had the shortest agenda I had ever cast my eyes over; in fact it carried just one item: 'Reduce the weekly wage bill of the contracted players from £15,000 to £5,000.' I told them with a straight face that they had to be joking.

They weren't however, and fifteen fights later, all I had managed to do was get them to agree to take it down to £6,000. That led to one of the most difficult times in my managerial career – can you imagine explaining to a player who had a contract and a mortgage to pay that the club wanted to claw back a chunk of their wages? Even so, we managed to get a team together for the start of the season.

The natives were restless though, as I had got rid of most of their highly-paid favourites and only three of the previous season's players had survived the cull. We lost our first game of the season 1-0 at home to Gravesend & Northfleet and jeers were ringing out at the final whistle. Things didn't really improve on the pitch over the next few weeks but I managed to begin a rejuvenation of the club's commercial arm by signing two major sponsors.

At the end of September we were drawn away in the second qualifying round of the FA Cup against Brockenhurst, a tiny team from the New Forest playing two levels of the pyramid below us in the Wessex League. Naturally, the travelling masses hadn't forgotten that Kingstonian's previous FA Cup tie just months earlier was a Fourth Round replay against Bristol City, for the right to play Premier League side Leicester City.

After a horrible performance – we were outplayed, out-fought and lost 2-1 after being a goal up – the boos were thunderous and some of the fans were baying for my blood.

Although we won the next league game 3-0 at home to Bedford Town, it was now October and after playing fourteen games, we had lost eight of them. The board called me in and rather than discuss the team's form (or rather lack of it), they told me that the club's financial problems had snowballed and that I needed to cut the budget even further.

As you can probably already gather, I have nothing amusing to say about my time at Kingstonian and I remember wondering where, oh where, had all the good times gone. I was also faced with a moral dilemma and found it hard to sleep at night knowing I was on a contract worth £50,000 a year while simultaneously being expected to pick my players' pockets.

So, for the first time in my career, I threw in the towel. To this day I'm still not sure who was the most relieved; me or the board. Likewise, from memory I'm not too sure if Mrs Williams was over the moon with my decision to abandon the security of a lucrative three-year-deal, but I had convinced myself (and Jill, of course!) that good money and a good contract were no good at all if you are not happy in your work.

My time at Kingstonian was, without doubt, my worst time in football management and sadly the club endured a financial nightmare for the next four or five years. I have thought about that job many times over the years and am sure that at the time there was never any real chance that I could have made the club a success – there were just too many money problems: they needed a good accountant, not a football manager. That said, I am absolutely delighted Kingstonian have come good in recent years as it was the club that I had supported as a youngster (along with Walton and Hersham, Newcastle United and Fulham).

No sooner had I left The K's the new chairman of Dover Athletic, Jim Gleeson, was on the phone explaining the terrible financial position the club was in and how, after just six months in the job, manager Gary Bellamy had been given the boot. Jim made it clear that he was not calling me for my football nous – he was on the verge of appointing former Wales and Everton goalkeeper Neville Southall as the new boss – but he wanted me to return to the club to help clear up the commercial mess that had hit the fan.

I accepted Jim's offer and soon realised that the current

squad needed thinning out: believe it or not some of the players were earning in excess of £600 a week and that certainly could not be sustained. Jim and I set about the nasty business which certainly wasn't anything new to me following my stint at Kingstonian. I couldn't help thinking, though, that footballing matters were now behind me and sorting out money problems was all I was left with. Whatever, we stabilised the budgets and Neville Southall took charge of the team. But little did I know the scale of disappointment and heartache that was waiting just around the corner...

Don't get me wrong, Neville Southall was a great goalkeeper. However, he really struggled as the manager of Dover and after losing nine of his first ten games in charge, the directors gave him the bullet. I need to make it clear here and now that I was not one of them.

Nevertheless, for some reason known only to himself, Neville spoke to the local newspapers and told them that the team's failure was not his fault at all but, believe it or not, down to me. I felt he was making excuses and I suppose he could have been misquoted, but come the next home game there were a dozen or so signs being held up around The Crabble all bearing the same stark message: WILLIAMS OUT.

It was a terrible feeling, largely because during the four years I had spent as the manager of Dover I felt I had enjoyed a very good rapport with the fans. My return to the south coast was clearly not a happy one and on reflection I wish that when I accepted control of the commercial side of the club, I should have insisted that I took charge of the team as well: at least if I'd got things wrong on the pitch, I could have taken the WILLIAMS OUT campaign on the chin.

Whatever, my working life became quite impossible at Dover after a Supporters' Trust took over the club and, as history shows, it was a decision that very near ruined them.

Personally, I was starting to have serious doubts about having anything to do with football whatsoever as the game, in my experience over the past few years, had become very stressful and seemingly all about money (or, to be specific, the lack of it). In my mind it was time to consider doing something outside of football, but I really didn't have much of a clue which way to turn.

Then, quite out of the blue, the secretary of Southern League side Welling United, Barrie Hobbins, was on the phone telling me that the club – which, incidentally, was formed by his father Sidney in 1963 to give Barrie and his brother, Graham, somewhere to play – was in trouble and he asked if I would be prepared to get the ship back on course.

I agreed to talk to them but arrived at the meeting carrying a sackful of trepidation, largely because each time I had previously met Graham, the general manager, we had only crossed swords. We first fell out when I was managing Maidstone and Graham was managing The Wings. Our relationship was soured further when I tried to buy Maidstone-born Andy Townsend from them in 1984 and then Graham tried to tuck me up on the purchase of John Bartley from us later the same year.

Regardless of the historical bad blood between us, I don't

think a meeting could have gone so well. Graham and Barrie were real football men and we realised that we had much in common. I therefore took the job as manager for the 2002/2003 season with a simple brief from the board – 'get the team into a mid-table position and we will be happy'.

Welling United was not a wealthy club by any stretch of the imagination, but they afforded themselves one luxury when they played away from home, by insisting on travelling First Class in one of the England team coaches and employing quality caterers. We always had a good day out, regardless of the result.

Then, as the season was ticking over nicely, I took a most surprising call from Bernard Baker, the former owner of the Barry Island Resort...

17

Viva España

YOU could have knocked me down with a soggy *Kent Messenger* when Bernard phoned, not least of all because he told me that he now had the money he owed me. He then went on to ask if I fancied running his new holiday villa business in Spain.

While obviously wondering if I could possibly trust him again after the Barry Island debacle, the proposition certainly gave me something to consider – should I stay in football and help out Welling, or help Jill pack our bags and set off together on a new voyage of discovery?

Towards the end of the 2002/2003 season, I was presented with a trophy for managing 1,500 professional games, which I received proudly. However, in need of a weekend away from football, Jill and I decided to fly to Spain to have a look around the Costa Blanca and check out the deal that Bernard was offering.

His offices were based in Calpe and we stayed in a beautiful villa overlooking the Mediterranean. We discovered that the first six villas had been built and were ready for rental and a further twenty four were on the production line. Jill and I had a wonderful weekend and we both felt no less excited about the project than we had during our adventures in South Africa and America. As such, the following week I told Barrie that I would finish the season at Welling and then call it a day.

It wasn't a particularly difficult decision: I had just turned sixty and knew I would not fulfil my dream of becoming a top Football League manager, so Jill and I decided it was a good idea to just enjoy whatever was coming to us.

Our initial plan was to spend one week in Spain and then two at home, which seemed sensible to me. There was much to do on the branding, marketing and sales side of the project so I drafted in two of the people who had helped me set up the Barry Island Resort. They needed to be paid in advance (of course!) but this time money was no obstacle as we had five major sponsors investing cash each month. Indeed, the working conditions were excellent and the future looked as bright as the Spanish sun.

My main job was to create enough enquiries to fill the thirty villas for the entire year. One day we were in Oliva trying to persuade one of the local letting agents to put our properties on their books, when football came up in the conversation. It turned out that the agent was the chairman of the local team and was looking for someone to take it off his hands.

In no time at all, we had been bitten by the Spanish

football fly and became the owners of UD Olivia, a non-league, part-time team six leagues away from the top flight in Spain. It was great to be involved in football again but overnight my workload had doubled.

The next couple of years felt rather like living in Heaven. The business was flying – agents were packing the villas to the rafters and the company was doing deals and buying up land all over the place – while the football team was running rings around the opposition. With plenty of family fun in the sun to boot, my latest throw of the dice had turned into a dream job.

Amid all of this working and playing hard, I was contacted by one of Maidstone United's directors, Ben McGannan, who was ringing on behalf of the club's chairman, Paul Bowden-Brown. They were hatching a plan to bring the club home to the town and wanted to know if I was interesting in getting involved. It was, of course, a no-brainer. I had a couple of weeks spare each month and still held Maidstone United dear to my heart. I therefore re-joined The Stones as a consultant offering advice on both the football side of things and ways to raise capital. As most readers will know, this project became an absolute passion for me over the following nine years.

Back on the Costa Packet, however, the markets began turning sharply in tune with the rest of the world and our investors' feet were getting itchy. They eventually decided to pull their money out completely and to compound the nightmare, we were told that half of the company's villas had been built illegally without the correct planning permission and the Spanish government had issued a demolition notice on four of them. Meanwhile, we had ploughed €250,000 into UD Oliva and, like all football clubs, they had found a way to spend the money quickly. Much of it had gone on buying new players but with all of it now frittered away, we received a request for cash to pay their wages as they were two weeks out of pocket. I'd seen all these signs before of course in both football and business and familiar red lights were flashing all over the place.

Anyway, two years earlier, a most beautiful chestnut and white cocker spaniel had hobbled into one of the company's sites just outside Oliva. She had been hit by a car and her leg was badly broken. Everyone said we should have her put down but between Jill, myself and the young lady who lived at and managed the site, we got her fixed up and her leg eventually mended. What we didn't know at the time was that she was carrying three extra passengers.

The reason for mentioning this touching case of animal rescue was that one day, the bitch and the pup that the site manager had kept from the litter came running out to greet me. The three of us sat down together and I know you will think I was losing my marbles, but they seemed to be asking for help. I therefore secured a small property for the young lady and her two dogs over the next few months, just in case the balloon went up.

And boy did it go up big time: all hell broke loose, with people chasing money from left, right and centre. I was in no way culpable, but I soon reached the conclusion that it was time to exit this bullring quicker than a naked matador.

18

Stoned Again

OUR time in Spain was a wonderful experience and should have lasted much longer, had the directors of the property company not been so stupid in purchasing swathes of worthless land. I still wonder to this day if it was all a giant con, and only last year I learnt from our accountants that the company went bust owing, believe it or not, a scorching €8.2 million.

With no financial background, I have, throughout my working life, left money matters to others, particularly those who are ploughing their own cash into the venture in question. However, if I had my time again I would definitely attend a couple of accountancy courses. I would also ask for my own budget and insist on having my side of the company ringfenced, because without wanting to sound too conceited, the departments I ran usually showed very healthy profits.

Looking back, the biggest deal I ever signed was the

contract to supply wheelchairs to the South African government, which was worth in excess of £10 million. By far the funniest, though, was the selling of Warren Barton to Wimbledon for £300,000.

Regardless of the pain in Spain, I was now back in Blighty full-time and ready to rekindle my love affair with Maidstone United Football Club. The romance had begun in 1972 and although I'd had a few drop-ins and drop-outs along the way, after thirty-five years it seemed that fate had somehow thrown us back together.

The proposal to Bring The Stones Home felt as though it would be the last major project of my life and a final mountain to climb, but could we really find the money and support to get Maidstone back to Maidstone? That, certainly, was the only way that the club could survive: ground-sharing with Sittingbourne and then Ashford was proving very unattractive for many fans and we were not getting the crowds we required at Bourne Park or Homelands. We did, of course, retain a large group of fervent supporters who had stayed loyal to the club after our demise in 1992, but they were too few to sustain the club's coffers. In short, finding investment to build a stadium in Maidstone was paramount.

A number of individuals and a couple of consortiums were approached – one of which went to great lengths to try to cut a deal – but sadly not one serious offer of involvement came forward for consideration.

On the plus side, the team was performing well on the pitch and had achieved back-to-back championships: the 2005/2006 season saw us win the Kent League title on the final day of the campaign, then under the joint leadership of Lloyd Hume and Alan Walker in 2006/2007, The Stones won the Isthmian League South at the first time of asking and gained promotion to the Isthmian Premier. And what wonderful days they were.

Another boost around this time came from local club South Park Rangers, who decided to bring their entire Under-12 operation over to MUFC. At the same time we amalgamated our own youth sides which suddenly made us a big club. In total, we were fielding twenty-eight teams but as they were all playing at different locations, a new stadium and headquarters were becoming ever more vital.

Then, in February 2008, up stepped a very tall, slim gentleman who told us that although he lived in Paris, he also had a home in Hythe and had been reading about our plight in the Kent newspapers and wanted to be involved. His name was Oliver Ash and he agreed to invest £120,000, which gave the club a new lease of life and chairman Paul Bowden-Brown a new director to work with.

Bowden-Brown had picked up the gauntlet following our demise in 1992 and had somehow managed to keep the club alive. Paul's football heart was certainly in the right place but, unfortunately, the same could not be said of his business brain. Money was dribbling in yet spilling out and the financial demands were causing major headaches, particularly for Paul's company, his health and his family. All the while the club was running out of both time and money and there were no more investors on the horizon. All those magical afternoons playing around the local pitches in the Kent League and then spreading our wings in the Isthmian South were quickly becoming distant memories as the club, for the second time in twenty-five years, was on the brink of extinction.

At home, meanwhile, James was now a strapping young man and had joined the local police force. Out one night enjoying all the trimmings of batchelor life, as you do, he met a smashing girl called Elizabeth. Then, blow me down, he announced something we never expected to hear – that Jill would need to order another new hat! James and Elizabeth were married at Aylesford Church on 3 May, 2008.

Back at the club, a thin ray of financial hope lay with the possible transfer of Chris Smalling to Middlesbrough. We had allowed Chris to remain an amateur while he played for England Youth, but despite him not being under contract, Middlesbrough were offering Chris a good package to get him to move up to the north east.

But, as we all know, Fulham's Director of Football Les Reed (who is now at Southampton) rocked up with Roy Hodgson, and we got a lesser deal from The Cottagers with Chris eventually being sold to Manchester United for £10million; a high-profile transfer deal which saw Maidstone United pick up sweet Fanny Adams in return.

After Chris signed for United I was invited up to Old Trafford to (finally) meet Sir Alex Ferguson. Jill asked if she could come along too, which was fine with me although I told her that she may not be invited to the meeting.

How wrong I was: Alex was the perfect host and while sitting with Jill and I he told stories from many of his experiences. He began by saying that he knew me through his good friend Craig Watson, and explained how they had started together at a youth club outside Glasgow. It made me think what a shame it was that the three of us weren't able to make that trip all those years ago. But it was a wonderful experience to meet the great Scot, and believe it or not Jill felt the same.

Despite getting to enjoy a glass of red with Sir Alex, the outcome of the Chris Smalling Affair saw a potential survival route for the club end in a cul-de-sac. Moreover, the club had seemingly reached the end of the road altogether, and an emergency meeting was called to break the news to the executive committee. I can still see the tears beginning to swell around the room at the prospect of the club not existing anymore. Oliver Ash and I duly resigned from the board and only Paul Bowden-Brown was left to attempt to control the impossible. As each day passed, the demise of Maidstone United drew closer. There were plenty of ideas being bandied about but, sadly, no hard and fast solutions.

To go into detail would take another book, but following many meetings and many hours of due diligence, lifelong supporter Terry Casey emerged through the fog on a white charger and offered to help save The Stones. Terry struck an agreement with Oliver in October 2010 and I was asked to join them (I believe some wag subsequently dubbed us 'The Holy Trinity'). It was decided that there would be no place or position for the out-going chairman and although that may seem harsh, it is common practice throughout the business world: if you put up the money, you want to control what happens to it.

It therefore came to the point when the proposal to save the club had to be put to the man who had at one time been instrumental in keeping it alive. Naturally, that was not a pleasant thing to do, but there was no alternative and looking at the state of the club today, the difficult decision was vindicated.

With Terry and Oliver's investment, preliminary work began on what was to become The Gallagher Stadium in August 2011. Full construction began at the end of September and £2.9 million later, turnstiles clicked in the county town for the first time in twenty four years on 14 July 2012. Finally, the Stones were home.

Our first season at the new ground was nothing short of monumental. Following the excitement of the grand opening against Brighton, manager Jay Saunders constructed a workmanlike side with splashes of flair that was only pipped to the Isthmian South title by Dulwich Hamlet's extra point. Nevertheless, following a tough and tense play-off semi-final victory over Folkestone Invicta, a balloon-strewn Gallagher Stadium was sold out for a superb 3-0 win over Faversham Town in the final and we were back in the Isthmian Premier.

Most significantly, though, home attendances had surged by a magnificent four-hundred-and-fifty per cent since our days at Bourne Park, with an average of 1,698 success-hungry fans turning up to cheer on the team. The unexpectedly high interest in the club's return to Maidstone meant that we could invest a further £50,000 in ground improvements in the summer of 2013. We also launched a Maidstone United Fan Club with Chris Smalling becoming the first member.

The close season also saw me make a surprise return to the dugout, twenty-two years after I had previously managed a Maidstone United team. I was asked to take charge of a squad of club directors, staff and sponsors for what was designed as the inaugural match in an annual cup showdown against a team of MUFC supporters. Mind you, I didn't really dig very deep into my bag of footballing tactics for the game, and the only piece of advice I offered my team beforehand was to make sure their life insurance was paid up and remind them that we were playing in amber.

It really had been an amazing return to the town, but I never dreamt in my wildest dreams that our comeback season would involve a teenage girl from The Stonettes dancing alongside Iggy the dinosaur while wearing a cardboard mask depicting my ugly mug.

Whatever, with the club seemingly on fire, and not in a Cardiff City Supporters' Bar kind of way, dare we dream that Maidstone United could one day return to the Football League? Well, as I've consumed the preceding pages glancing at the past, I'd like to spend a few words looking into the future...

19

Rockin' on Heaven's Door

IT GOES without saying that after fifty-odd years of marriage, there are many things for which I have Jill to thank. We've had lovely children, enjoyed a wonderful life together and, as you've read, she has allowed me to follow my footballing dreams and chase my business ideas around the globe, supporting me in whatever I've decided to do. Even on Barry Island. However, I will always be eternally grateful to my dear wife for particularly being my best friend over a couple of weeks at the end of August 2010...

Sandwiched between the bills, bank statements and endless invitations to have pizza delivered, I found on the doormat around that time a screening test for bowel cancer, addressed to yours truly. It arrived as part of a national campaign championing the benefits of early detection but, to be honest, I was probably more alarmed by the fact that you could now have the crust of your deep-pan stuffed with hot dogs. Mrs W, on the other hand, immediately grasped the nettle and spent the following fortnight nagging me to take the test until I finally caved in.

I won't go into detail about how the assessment is performed, just in case you're eating your tea, but I popped the screening kit into its special envelope and sent it off to the laboratory. The results came back three weeks later marked 'abnormal', meaning blood had been found in my samples.

Two months, a couple of endoscopies, a CT scan and many blood tests later, I found myself sitting in front of Mr Rakesh Bhardwaj, the bowel cancer specialist at Darent Valley Hospital in Dartford. Looking me squarely in the eye, Mr Bhardwaj told me I had malignant polyps and that part of my colon needed to be removed. By nature I had been expecting the worst but it came as a real shock and I can still hear those dreaded words 'I have cancer' ringing inside my head. I could've picked up my guitar there and then and learnt the chords to *Knockin' On Heaven's Door*.

Now, plenty of people are perfectly comfortable with being admitted to hospital and undergoing surgery, but I can tell you that I am certainly not one of those. Quite the reverse, in fact – I suffer from 'white coat syndrome', which effectively means that if a nurse or doctor comes within twelve square football pitches of me, my blood pressure shoots through the roof and I sweat like Lee Evans in a Turkish bath.

So, as you can imagine, following the diagnosis I had just received and a detailed description of the treatment I required, the big, brave Bill that you know and put up with was anything but big and brave.

Anyone who has contracted the same or a similarly nasty disease will know that you are never in short supply of reassuring souls saying: 'Don't worry, you'll be alright.' But when they said it to me it went in one ear and straight out of the other and I got so worried about the op, I told Jill I didn't think I could go through with it. I can't tell you exactly what she said but it was very much along the lines of: 'Pull yourself together and man-up – that's what you've always been very good at telling others to do.'

Regardless, while realising that the only way I could spend a bit more time on Earth was to face the operation, my mind was telling me that I needed some professional help in order to go under the knife. So off I went to see a hypnotherapist.

I had five sessions with Mandy Shepherd at Bluebird Hypnotherapy but didn't feel any positive effects. At the final session I told her that I couldn't see how my weekly trip to 'dreamland' would quell my fears. Nevertheless, Mandy asked me to telephone her after the operation to let her know how it had gone.

People had told me before – but I now know first hand – that when you are going into hospital for major surgery, your mind can play tricks on you. In the eight months between being told that I needed the operation, agreeing to it and arriving at hospital in May 2011, I must have considered all the possible outcomes a hundred times and found it annoying to think of the things I still wanted to do but maybe didn't have time to do.

Nick drove Jill and I to the hospital. I was pretty relaxed – I had to keep the 'hard man' image going – but I knew that once I saw the hospital my heart would start racing.

'Come this way, Mr Williams, and say goodbye to your family,' said the nurse. I asked her if she could possibly re-phrase her request, ideally without using the word 'goodbye'.

So on the trolley I laid with needles in my arm and back, ready to be wheeled into the operating theatre. I turned to the nurse and asked her how high my blood pressure was. 'It's absolutely perfect Mr Williams,' she said. I told her it couldn't possibly be 'perfect'. She simply repeated her answer and I went into the operation of my life totally relaxed, thinking that the hypnotist had done a wonderful job of easing my mind. I mustn't forget to write to her.

I cannot express in words the wonderful treatment I received at Darent Valley Hospital under the NHS: everyone was brilliant and I can never thank them enough. I was one of the lucky ones – problem detected early, operation successful and I only need to go and see my specialist once a year which I hope very soon will revert to once every three years.

So I'm still rockin' and not quite ready to shuffle off this mortal coil just yet. There is of course plenty of work to do at MUFC and I am determined to see both my granddaughters walk up the aisle.

As far as Maidstone United Football Club is concerned, had Terry and Oliver not shouldered the debt left by the previous regime and then shelled out a fortune for the new stadium, I think I can safely say that we would no longer exist. It therefore goes without saying that every single supporter of the football club owes both men a great debt of gratitude.

At the time of writing, we have been in operation for eighteen months. Our average gate has risen to 1,875 and our first year's accounts showed a very healthy profit of more than £180,000. But far more amazing to me is the fact that it feels as if the whole of the county town and indeed some of the surrounding areas have come along and supported what we are trying to achieve in a number of different ways, be it buying advertising space, hiring the pitch or the Spitfire Lounge or patronising the Development Centres. Blimey, even our planning application was supported by the council.

The stadium has provided a wonderful outlet for the local community and it's fantastic how successful each separate section of the business has become. The big question is: how far can the current ownership take the club?

Terry and Oliver are both very sensible men and will only venture forward as long as it can be seen to be cost effective (although they were, of course, prepared to gamble three million in the first place).

But now that the Conference has been strong-armed by the FA into accepting 3G as a legitimate playing surface, you could say the sky's the limit. And when you bear in mind that the population of Maidstone is similar in size to Reading or Norwich, if you say it quickly there is no reason why Maidstone couldn't eventually support a Championship team.

We will gauge the volume of support the club garners over the seasons and develop the ground as demand requires. This is already happening of course – in readiness for a hopeful promotion to the Conference South Terry has unveiled a £500,000 scheme to extend the main stand, adding 350 seats to the ground capacity.

But who really knows? In five years' time we could be top of the Conference, playing to a 5,000-plus crowd on the brink of promotion back into the Football League. And in another ten years, the club could be in the First Division playing to 15,000 and on the cusp of the Championship. It does, however, all come down to money and although things don't always pan out the way you'd like even if you do have access to sufficient funds, you can usually find a way.

Given time and a fair wind – which is another way of saying enough dosh – I think Maidstone United will find themselves back in the Football League. How far up the leagues they can progress will depend on whether the club can attract a wealthy benefactor or build mammoth support. Or, preferably, both.

Well, that's it really; I think we're pretty much up-to-date. I'm off to the Gallagher to launch Bill's Big Bonanza. Yeehaw.

The only thing left for me to address is the small matter of who they cast as me when this book is made into a film (ahem). Believe it or not, when I was playing for Mansfield, the lads nicknamed me 'Gene': not because I danced like Gene Kelly, delivered a punchline like Gene Wilder or stuck my tongue out while playing the guitar like Gene Simmons out of Kiss, but because they insisted I was a deadringer for Gene Hackman.

I can't really see it myself. Des Lynam, perhaps...

Postscript

The nice lady at the printers has asked me to stop blathering now, as she's about to put this book to bed. And who can blame her for wanting to do that. But there is, in the words of Lieutenant Columbo, just one more thing...

As we go to print, Elizabeth and James are due to become parents at any moment. The family is filled with joy and excitement, naturally, and I just can't help wondering if my branch of the Williams' tree will survive after all, with the sprouting of a little skipper...

Editor's note:
Alan James Williams was born on 13 October, 2014.

Appendix I

My All Time Greatest MUFC XI

MANY fine players have made the amber shirt sweaty for Maidstone United over the years and I have often been asked who would fill the team-sheet in my ideal side. So for the record, here they are with my reasons for their selection.

BEENEY

THOMPSON   SMALLING   NEWSON   BARTON

ASHFORD   SORRELL

GALL   TAYLOR

BUTLER   BARTLEY

MARK BEENEY (1987-1991)

Standing six feet four inches tall and weighing in at fourteen and a half stones, Mark was the perfect build for what most coaches look for in a goalkeeper. He was exceptionally agile for a big man and had a safe pair of hands but in his early days with us he wasn't as commanding in the box as I would have liked. He did however work on that aspect of his game which saw him snapped up by Brighton and Hove Albion for £200,000 in 1991 before Leeds United signed him two years later as back-up to John Lukic and then Nigel Martyn.

One outstanding save Mark made that springs to mind was during a Gillingham derby game at Priestfield: a powerful free-kick in the second half was bent around the wall and Mark stretched every muscle to fingertip the ball past the post.

After retiring Mark went into football management with Sittingbourne but resigned in 2004 to become a goalkeeping coach at Chelsea where his son, Mitchell, stands between the posts for their under 21s.

CHRIS SMALLING (2007-2008)

Chris was brought to Maidstone by former manager Peter Knott and I can remember the day of his trial, which was at the now defunct ground at Snodland Working Men's Club.

Chris was clearly very tall and I'd seen more fat on a butcher's pencil. He was also sporting an outrageous afro, which made him look like a young Michael Jackson on stilts. But despite his looks, it was his athleticism and silky football skills that made him stand out from the crowd that day.

Chris was always destined for the big time, but I'm sure none of us at the time would ever in our wildest dreams have imagined he would be on the plane with the full England squad to play in the World Cup in Brazil. He came to us by chance, largely because his mother insisted that he finish his education before taking up football. Even though Millwall let him go when he was fifteen, I do believe he would have come through the ranks there.

Chris is a lovely lad and deserves the chance that life and football has given him and of course I am immensely proud to have played a small part in his development.

BRIAN THOMPSON (1981-1985)

With the exception of Malcolm Stewart and Tony Sorrell, Brian is the most uncompromising player to turn out for The Stones during my time at the club. You knew exactly what you would get from him each week and so, to their regret, did the opposition.

Brian came to us from Mansfield Town and was a very fit, quick, all-action player. Although a full-back by trade, he was extremely versatile and equally comfortable in a man-for-man marking role or playing in a central back-three unit picking up the quickest forward.

Brian always professed that there wasn't a forward in the league who could beat him for speed and on the rare occasions when one came along who could, they invariably found themselves dumped on the greyhound track at the Athletic Ground.

Although he was the only player I ever had to fine for

committing a career-threatening tackle on an opponent, Brian was a very intelligent and likeable young man and following some outstanding performances for the club, he represented his country numerous times at semi-professional international level.

MARK NEWSON (1979-1985)

Mark was at the club when I arrived in 1981 and was a young midfielder who had been given a free transfer from Charlton Athletic. I soon converted him into a central defender where his exceptional pace, balance and close control made him stand out in what at the time was a very talented side.

Mark won five caps for his country as a semi-pro before moving to Harry Redknapp's Bournemouth in a very controversial transfer: Barry Fry had let him come off a contract so that Mark could coach in the States, so Bournemouth duly bagged him without parting with a penny. (According to Harry, Barry and Jim Thompson were so incensed, they allegedly pitched up at Dean Court with Mr Another threatening to separate Harry from his kneecaps.)

Mind you, it wasn't the first time Mark had messed about with his contract: when I first took him on as a professional, he signed the form as 'Paul Newman', which wasn't picked up until the paperwork reached the FA.

Mark was a great competitor and played in the Football League for a several years before becoming a coach at West Ham United and Crystal Palace.

WARREN BARTON (1989-1990)

Next to Chris Smalling, Peter Taylor and David Sadler – who doesn't make my All Time Greatest XI even though he played 335 times for Manchester United and a few games for England! – Warren is our most famous player.

He was recommended to me by John Still but to be honest I wasn't sure about him when I first watched him play at Redbridge. However, John threatened to knock me out if I didn't sign him which swayed my opinion somewhat. And John was quite right – from his first game, at Peterborough, Warren was tremendously exciting and very popular with the fans. His speed made him hard to beat and a threat coming forward plus he had energy to burn and flair in the final third.

Warren wasn't the toughest tackler or the swiftest in the air, but he certainly had something as Wimbledon, Newcastle United and England will confirm. During his career, Warren commanded more than £4.5 million in transfer fees.

NOEL ASHFORD (1988-1989)

This may spark some heated debate in the Spitfire Lounge, but in my opinion Noel was the most talented player ever to turn out for the club and to this day I am still baffled why he was never picked up a big pro outfit.

The reason for rating him so highly is that he played in that very difficult position just behind the strikers; a similar linking position between midfield and the forwards that Wayne Rooney adopts for the other MUFC. He had everything and his timing while making runs from midfield to weigh in with his quota of goals was quite brilliant at times.

If Noel had a weakness it was his total lack of ambition, which was such a shame considering his abundance of skill. He played many times for the England semi-professional team but when we won promotion to the Football League and the club went full-time, Noel left to play semi-pro elsewhere.

TONY SORRELL (1989-1991)

Tony was one of those unsung heroes whose name was always first on my team-sheet. A tough ball-winner with tight control and passing ability, he was also a tremendous athlete and exceptional in the air.

The only problem with Tony was that he had the temper of Vesuvius and would blow his top when no one was expecting it. Indeed, from memory, I think in the time he was with us he accounted for half our disciplinary problems personally.

Tony's massive long throws were as effective as a free kick and we scored many goals from second-ball situations. Tony also chipped in with a goal himself on occasions, and one that particularly sticks in my mind was during our 1-1 FA Cup draw at Reading in December 1988, when Tony, on the end of a deep Mark Gall cross, hung in the air for what seemed like ages before bulleting a header into the top corner.

MARK GALL (1988-1991)

In the 133 times he turned out for The Stones, Mark scored a remarkable seventy-one goals. Considering that the club paid just £2000 to bring him from Greenwich Borough, he is without doubt one of best purchases we've ever made and his goal tally – twenty-six in twenty five starts in 1988/1989 – was instrumental in the club gaining promotion to the Football League. He had the pace of a lightning bolt and was as strong and fearless as a bull but, above all else, he had a variety of finishes and could score volleys, chips and drives with either foot and was also no slouch in the air.

We eventually sold Mark for £45,000 to Brighton and Hove Albion, where he netted thirteen goals in thirty-one appearances before rupturing his medial ligament. Following surgery and specialist advice, Mark was forced to retire from the game and the Brixton boy returned to London to work in the family bakery.

STEVE BUTLER (1986-1991)
The yang to Mark Gall's yin, Steve was a fantastic striker and they formed a stunning partnership. I'm not sure if we got him from Brentford or the army, but what I can remember is seeing him play for an Army XI in Aldershot after his family, who lived locally, had recommended him to the club.

For a tall man – well over six feet – Steve possessed superb control and was equally at home as a target or playing slightly behind the front man. Steve had a very high level of stamina which no doubt came from the training he did as a PTI in the forces. His other great skill was scoring goals; many of them spectacular.

Yet he will always be remembered (sorry, Steve) for the chance he missed in the Third Round of the FA Cup tie at Sheffield United when, with the score at 0-0 in the second half, he rounded the keeper and with the goal at his mercy, blazed the ball wide.

Nevertheless, Steve played a major part in our promotion to the Football League (twenty-six goals in thirty-eight starts in 1988/1989) and put in some great performances in the Fourth Division, until we accepted an offer of £150,00 for his services from Watford. As a UEFA qualified coach, it was no surprise when he joined Peter Taylor as his assistant at Leicester, Gillingham and Hull when he finished playing.

Steve, incidentally, is the only player who would (and still does) call me Mr Williams: once an army man, always an army man!

JOHN BARTLEY (1982-1984, 1986-1987)

Netting 85 goals in 114 games, John had the hottest boots in my time managing The Stones. His claim to fame was notching a hundred hat-tricks in senior football, a fact that earned him a garage full of footballs and me many a pint in football bars around the country.

Standing five feet eight and weighing a good thirteen stones, John was a most unlikely looking striker but with the ball at his feet his power and pace were phenomenal. With a natural eye for goal and a range of finishes available from either foot, he was very much like 'Smokey' Gall but I would say John was just a little bit more accurate. He scored some great goals, some tap-ins and some flew in off his shins, but John could always bag you a goal if the chips were down.

The one that stands out for me was a brilliant opportunist effort in the 90th minute of the 1983/1984 Championship decider against Nuneaton Borough: we had been hammered for much of the game but had them held at 1-1 when John turned sharply in the box and drilled a low drive into the corner. (For precisely one minute we had the Alliance League title in our grasp, until we conceded an equaliser in the second minute of time added on. Still, we did, of course, thump Telford 6-0 to become champions five days later.)

I got John on a free transfer from Helsinki but when he began to put on more weight, I fell out with him and sold him back to Welling.

PETER TAYLOR (1982-1983, 1984-1986)
One of the very few full internationals to play for Maidstone, Peter was the ultimate crowd pleaser. You could give him the ball when you were under pressure and rely on him to hold on to it and take on a couple of defenders while the rest of the team got their shape back.

His tight control and body swerve – and, of course, his passing across ten yards – were a feature of his game. His crossing and dead-ball delivery was also tremendous and he would score his fair share of goals. Peter is up there with the very best that have played for us and I'm proud to say he got the coaching bug while working on set pieces when I was in charge (and that I normally took the credit for!).

Peter has of course gone on to reach great heights in coaching and management and can you imagine writing 'Managed England' on your CV? He also has a wicked sense of humour – which sadly doesn't always come across on TV – and does the best impression of Norman Wisdom I have ever seen.

... and what a bench!

KENNY HILL (1976-1983)

When my full-time professional career finished at Gillingham, it was Kenny who took my place at the centre of defence, although it wasn't until I returned to manage Maidstone in 1981 that I met up with him again. He had for a few seasons been part of an outstanding central partnership with Neil Merrick and was coming towards the end of his career, which was celebrated in April 1983 with a testimonial against Manchester City.

Great in the air and the ultimate warrior – '*Six foot two/ Eyes of blue/Kenny Hill is after you*' the lads in the Shed at London Road would sing – Kenny was frightened of nothing as the scars on his head bear witness. His reading of the game and his organisational skills were excellent and he was the perfect type of defender for the Conference and I'm still surprised that Kenny didn't stay in the game, as he had tremendous leadership skills.

CHRIS KINNEAR (1977-1981)

Equally at home on the right or the left, Chris was primarily an attacking player who could slot comfortably into a wing-back position when called upon.

A schoolteacher by profession, Chris was a keen student of the game and it was no surprise when he excelled as a manager when his playing days were over.

His main attributes were a clever use of the ball and good crossing ability, which set up many chances over the years. Chris' stamina levels were admirable and he knew how to defend properly. He was always a very quiet member of the dressing room and only piped up if the subject turned to tactical decisions, when, on reflection, he would have quite a lot to say.

When I came to the club as manager in 1981 I brought with me from the States the sweeper system that I had employed abroad, and it is interesting that Chris has used a similar formation throughout his managerial career which has brought him great success.

JOHN GLOVER (1984-1988)

One afternoon I took a call from Graham Carr, who at the time was managing Nuneaton Borough. 'I've got the best centre-half in semi-pro football and you can have him for £2000 as he's moving to Maidstone with his job,' he said. Having only been back in Britain for a short while I had no idea who John Glover was and thought it was a wind-up, but after a few conversations with people whose opinion I respected, I realised this was a real deal on the table. I therefore went to see him play at Nuneaton and signed him on the spot.

It was a great piece of business as John was an outstanding defender and would dominate all aerial battles. University trained, he was super-fit and became another of our semi-pro internationals.

The one story I will always remember about John was when we were about to play one of our many top-of-the-table clashes against Enfield at home: half-an-hour before the game he still hadn't reported in, when he phoned asking where I was. I told him I was at the ground waiting for him and he said he was at the ground waiting for me. Trouble was, I, the rest of the team and the supporters were in Maidstone, and he was in Enfield; it seems the one course he didn't take at university was the one titled Common Sense

John was a lovely man and we kept in touch over the years, until his very sad death in 2006 at the age of just 51.

FRANK OVARD (1979-1981, 1982-1985)

An out-and-out left winger, Frank was totally unique and a real character. His ability when running at opponents was frightening, not least of all for them. I'm not entirely convinced he always knew what he was doing, but on the same count neither did the opposition and Frank invariably found a way to put in a cross, score a goal or win a penalty. He had very close control and it seemed the ball was glued to his boot.

Although I shouldn't admit it, Frank was the first player I saw in semi-pro football who had perfected what FIFA now label 'simulation': indeed, some say Frank was more fond of a dive than Captain Nemo.

He hated defending which unfortunately cost us a huge FA Cup tie at Weymouth in 1982: after being 3-1 up, Frank let the full back run onto us and the right back hung two rockets in the roof of the net before crossing the ball for the winner which saw us beaten 4-3.

Frank – who didn't drive but was always on time for training and matches – was sold to Gillingham for £10,000, where he made a handful of appearances. Yet he soon returned to London Road, much to the delight of our fans.

Appendix II

Bill Williams' Career

HERE'S a summary of what I did, when I did it and who I did it for. As you can see, as a player I was not what you would call a prolific scorer of goals. Mind you, I didn't half stop a few.

SENIOR CAREER

		Appearances	Goals
1960-1961	Portsmouth	3	0
1961-1963	Queens Park Rangers	48	0
1964-1965	West Bromwich Albion	1	0
1965-1967	Mansfield Town	51	0
1967-1972	Gillingham	189	8
1972-1973	Maidstone United	26	3
1973-1974	Durban Celtic	12	1
1974-1976	Durban United	27	2

ENGLAND UNDER 18s

Appearances	Goals
8	0

MANAGERIAL CAREER

1973-1974	Durban Celtic
1974-1975	Durban United
1975-1979	Durban City
1979-1980	Sacramento Gold
1980-1982	Atlanta Chiefs
1982-1985	Maidstone United
1985-1986	Durban United
1986-1992	Maidstone United
1996-2001	Dover Athletic
2001-2002	Kingstonian
2002-2003	Welling United

Index